INSPIRED

HOW TO CREATE PRODUCTS CUSTOMERS LOVE

Marty Cagan

TABLE OF CONTENTS

Part III – Product..175

Summary...215

INTRODUCTION

In the mid 1980s, I was a young software developer working for HP on a high-profile product. It was when Artificial Intelligence was all the rage, and I was fortunate enough to be working at one of the industry's best companies, as part of a very strong software engineering team (several members of that team went on to substantial success in companies across the industry). Our assignment was a difficult one: to deliver software on a low-cost, general-purpose workstation that until then required a special-purpose hardware/software combination that cost over $100,000 per user—a price few could afford.

We worked long and hard for well over a year, sacrificing countless nights and weekends. Along the way, we added several patents to HP's portfolio. We developed the software to meet HP's exacting quality standards. We internationalized the product and localized it for several languages. We trained the sales force. We previewed our technology with the press and received excellent reviews. We were ready. We released. We celebrated the release.

Just one problem: No one bought it.

The product was a complete failure in the marketplace. Yes, it was technically impressive, and the reviewers loved it, but it wasn't something people wanted or needed.

The team was of course frustrated with this outcome. But soon we began to ask some important questions: Who decides what products we should actually build? How do they decide? How do they know that what we build will be useful?

Our young team learned something very profound—something I'm sure many teams have discovered the hard way: *It doesn't matter how good your engineering team is if they are not given something worthwhile to build.*

More generally, we learned that it's not enough to do a good job engineering a product. At least as important is *discovering a product that is valuable, usable, and feasible.*

When trying to track down the root cause of our failure, I learned that the decisions about what to build came from a "Product Manager"—someone who generally resided in the marketing organization and who was responsible for defining the products we built. But I also learned that Product Management wasn't something HP was particularly good at. I later learned that most companies weren't good at this, and in fact most still aren't.

I promised myself that never again would I work so hard on a product unless I knew the product would be something that users and customers wanted.

Over the next 20 years, I had the very good fortune to work on some of the most successful high-tech products of our time—first at HP during the rise of personal computers, then at Netscape Communications/AOL during the rise of the Internet where I served as vice-president of platform and tools, and finally at eBay during the rise of e-commerce where I served as the senior vice-president of product management and design.

Not all of the product efforts have been as successful as others, but I am happy to say that none were failures, and several became loved and used by millions of people around the world.

Soon after I left eBay, I started getting calls from product organizations wanting to improve how they produced products. As I began working with these companies, I discovered that there was a tremendous difference between how the *best* companies produced products, and how *most* companies produced them. I realized that *the state of the art was very different from the state of the practice.* Most companies were still using old and inefficient ways to define and create products. I also discovered that there was precious little help available, either from academia, including the best business school programs, or from industry organizations, which seemed hopelessly stuck in the failed models of the past—just like the one I worked in at HP.

I have had some great rides, and I am especially thankful that I have had the chance to work for and with some of the best product minds in the industry. The best ideas in this book are from these people. You will find a list of many of them in the acknowledgements. I have learned from them all and I am grateful to each one of them.

I chose this career because I wanted to work on products that customers love; products that inspire and provide real value. I find that most product leaders also want to create inspiring and successful products. Yet most products are not inspiring, and life is too short for bad products.

My hope in writing this book is that it will help share the best practices of the most successful product companies, and that the result will be more products that are truly inspiring—products that customers love.

Who This Book Is For

This book is specifically written for those members of *software product teams*—especially Internet software product teams—both consumer and business, who are *responsible for defining the products to be built.* Often these product leaders are called "product managers," but they may be company founders, executives, lead engineers, or designers.

In addition to product managers, this book is for user experience designers, software engineers and architects, project/program managers, product marketing managers, and the managers of the different parts of the product organization.

In my experience, the information described here is applicable to a wide variety of product development teams:

Your company may be a startup, or a very large business with many products, or something in between. You may be working on an all-new 1.0 product, or working on incremental improvements to an existing product. Your product development team may be using an *Agile* method such as *Scrum,* or conventional Waterfall-based methods.

Your product may be an Internet service, shipped software, a device, or a platform. It may be for consumers, small businesses, or enterprises. For instance, the products could be e-commerce Web sites, fantasy sports or game sites, consumer electronics, hosted services for businesses, or platforms for enabling specific types of Internet applications and services such as social networking or video sharing.

One caveat I have to make is that the book is not intended for those working on non-software products, such as pharmaceuticals, and also for non-product software efforts, such as custom software projects. That's not to say that the methods and strategies I describe won't work in other environments, but I developed these concepts and practiced them in the product software world, so they may not be as effective outside of it.

How This Book Is Structured

When I first moved into senior management roles at Netscape, I found my day-to-day tasks fell into three distinct areas: *People, Process,* and *Product:*

Great Products by Design

I do not believe inspiring products happen by accident. In every case, behind every successful, inspiring product, I find that there are certain truths. Here are ten such truths that I try to keep in mind on every product effort:

1. The job of the product manager is to *discover* a product that is valuable, usable, and feasible.

2. Product discovery is a collaboration between the product manager, interaction designer, and software architect.

3. Engineering is important and difficult, but user experience design is even more important, and usually more difficult.

4. Engineers are typically very poor at user experience design— engineers think in terms of implementation models, but users think in terms of conceptual models.

5. User experience design means both interaction design and visual design (and for hardware-based devices, industrial design).

6. Functionality (product requirements) and user experience design are inherently intertwined.

7. Product ideas must be tested—early and often—on actual target users in order to come up with a product that is valuable and usable.

8. We need a high-fidelity prototype so we can quickly, easily, and frequently test our ideas on real users using a realistic user experience.

9. The job of the product manager is to identify the *minimal* possible product that meets the objectives—valuable, usable and feasible—minimizing time to market and user complexity.

10. Once this minimal successful product has been discovered and validated, it is not something that can be piecemealed and expect the same results.

I continue to talk to far too many product teams stuck in old, failed ways of creating products. Coming to terms with these truths is what this book is all about.

People refers to the product organization, and the roles and responsibilities of the members of the team as they define and develop the product.

Process refers to the processes, activities and best practices used to repeatedly discover and build inspiring and successful products.

Product refers to the defining characteristics of these inspiring products.

All three of these areas are essential to discovering and creating inspiring products. Everything starts with the people, but the process is what enables these people to consistently produce inspiring and successful products.

I have organized this book into these same three parts. Each part is broken up into several independent topics. The order within each of these parts is generally not important—you can jump from one topic to another. Each topic is meant to be self-contained. At the end of the book, I sum everything up by describing what I think are the 10 most important practices and techniques.

Many of the topics discussed in this book reveal the best practices applied by some of the best companies in the world. Others are based on interviews with some of the best product minds in our industry. And yet others are based on my own experiences in the companies I have worked for and with.

Remember: This book is only useful if it helps you deliver better products, so the intention is for each and every topic to be thought provoking, relevant, and actionable.

It is my hope that this information will help you create more successful products, and I would love to hear about your experiences. Please visit me online at the Silicon Valley Product Group site (www.svpg. com) and let me know what you think.

Here's to your success, and to the discovery of inspiring products that customers love.

 Examples

I am a big believer in the power of examples, both good and bad. But, because our industry changes so quickly, one of the challenges in a book like this is providing timely and relevant examples. Another problem is that including my favorite examples would add more than one hundred extra pages to this book.

I therefore put many of the examples on the Silicon Valley Product Group web site (www.svpg.com/examples). This way I can continue to update and add to the examples without needing to update the content of the book. As with all of the material on the site, there is no fee or registration required.

The online examples include opportunity assessments, product principles, product strategies, product roadmaps, product specs, prototypes, personas, and prototype testing questions and tasks.

I apologize that this means that you will need Internet access to see many of the examples, and I realize that this breaks the flow of reading a book, but I hope you find the benefits of this approach outweigh the inconvenience.

You will find references in the chapters that follow to the examples on the site.

DILBERT: © Scott Adams/Dist. by United Feature Syndicate, Inc.

The Product Organization

Every product begins with the people on the product team. How you define the roles, and who you select to staff the team, will very likely prove to be a determining factor in its success or failure.

In this section we will describe the key roles and responsibilities of modern software and Internet product teams.

This is an area where many product teams fall short, stuck in old models of the past. For many organizations the roles and responsibilities discussed here represent significant differences from what they're used to.

Chapter 1:

KEY ROLES AND RESPONSIBILITIES

The Modern Software Product Organization

Throughout this book I'll be referencing the key roles on the product team, and in this first chapter I will define exactly what I mean by each. I realize that not every company uses these titles or assigns the responsibilities in exactly this way, but I believe the most successful companies do, and that each of these roles is essential to creating successful products.

Remember that when I say "software product organization" I'm referring to not just shipped software for business or consumers, but also Internet or web services for businesses or consumers, and consumer electronics or other software-centric devices.

Product Manager

The product manager has two key responsibilities: assessing product opportunities, and defining the product to be built. Typically, new ideas can come from anywhere—company executives, discussions with customers, usability testing, your own product team, your sales or marketing staff, industry analysts, to name a few. But then someone needs to take a hard look at the idea and decide if it is something worth pursuing. The product manager is responsible for this assessment (many companies call this an MRD—Market

Requirements Document—but I'll describe a lighter-weight version of this called an Opportunity Assessment).

Once you've decided that you have a good opportunity and your company is well-suited to pursue it, then someone needs to *discover* what the solution—the product—actually is, including the necessary features and functionality, the user experience, and the release criteria. Again, this someone is the product manager, and this task is the heart of his or her job. Some companies call this spec a Product Requirements Document (PRD), and others call it a Product Spec or Functional Spec. Again, I'll advocate a lighter-weight approach that's based on prototypes and not paper, but the key is that it describes the functionality and behavior of the product to be built, and not how it will be implemented.

User Experience Designer

There are actually several roles within the user experience design organization and I'll dive into more detail later on each of these. The key role here is the interaction designer (also known as information architect, user interface designer, and user experience architect). These people are responsible for developing a deep understanding of the target users (each persona that you're trying to satisfy in your product), and coming up with the tasks, navigation, and flow that are both usable and productive. The interaction designer works closely with the product manager to discover the blend of requirements and design that meet the needs of the user. The idea is to get to the point where the software is both usable (users can figure out how to use it) and valuable (users actually want to use it).

Project Management

Once the product has been defined, the product development team will take on the project and begin building the product. The project scheduling and tracking function is the core of project management. There are several different models regarding who exactly handles the scheduling and tracking. Sometimes it is managed by dedicated project managers, sometimes by the engineering manager (since most of the resources are usually from his or her team), and in some cases the product manager is asked to project manage as well. It often depends more on the culture of the company and the size of the project. Larger projects especially benefit from a dedicated and skilled project manager.

Engineering

Also known as product development or software developers these are the people responsible for actually building the product. In some companies this is called "IT" (information technology), but it's important to draw a distinction between the software created for customers and the software created for internal use such as an HR application. IT is typically the group that supports internal employees, and the engineering organization builds and maintains products for external customers.

 What About Agile Teams?

Many of the product organizations I work with are using some form of *Agile* Methods, in particular, the most popular called *Scrum*. If you haven't heard of these, I cover them more in depth in the chapter *Succeeding with Agile Methods*.

In most *Scrum* software organizations, the product manager serves as the *Product Owner*, and the project manager typically serves as the *ScrumMaster*. The other roles defined earlier are essentially the same.

There are, however, several very important considerations for *Agile* teams when it comes to product organizations, such as incorporating user experience design, and managing the release process, and we will discuss these points throughout the book.

Site Operations

For Internet services, the product is typically run on central servers and accessed over the Web. The site operations team is responsible for keeping this service running. While some companies ask the engineering team to cover this, most find that it demands a specialized set of skills and is far too important to be a secondary responsibility.

Product Marketing

The product marketing team member is responsible for telling the world about the product, managing the external-facing product launch, providing tools for the sales channel to market and sell the product, and for leading key programs such as online marketing campaigns and influencer marketing programs. Often companies ask the same person to cover both the product management (product definition) and the product marketing responsibilities. This can be difficult since the skills required are very different, but nevertheless it occurs at many companies.

Side Note: At Microsoft, the people that define the product and drive the project schedule are called program managers, which is an unfortunate title given that the term is already widely used in the industry to describe multiple-team project management. However, they could not use the term product manager either because they already use that to represent the product marketing function. While I wish they would use different titles (for both), in general I think they do a very good job on the critical product management role of defining products.

What Are The Right Ratios of Roles?

In any software product organization, you will find that there are some natural ratios between product managers, designers and engineers. This is because to keep a particular engineering team busy with valuable and usable software to build, there is a certain amount of work that the product managers and designers must do (and therefore a certain number of people in these positions) to support the engineers.

There are of course several other factors that influence the right ratio of roles, such as the type of software being produced, and the experience and skill of the staff, but the ratios that follow should give you a guideline.

Q: How many product managers do we need?

A: Generally, one product manager for every 5-10 engineers.

Q: How many user experience designers do we need?

A: One interaction designer can generally support two product managers, and one visual designer can typically support four interaction designers.

Q: Should we have dedicated project managers?

A: For significant-sized projects, such as those with more than 5 engineers, yes. Further, if you use the "train model" of releases (where you make a release every one to four weeks consistently, and if a given feature is not ready it simply moves to the next available train), you'll definitely need dedicated project managers assigned to each release (which generally contains software from multiple projects).

Chapter 2:

PRODUCT MANAGEMENT VS. PRODUCT MARKETING

They Are Not The Same Thing

Industry pundits claim that as much as nine out of ten product releases are failures in that they fail to meet their objectives. Even if your organization performs better than this, I strongly believe that most releases are ill-conceived. Countless release cycles are wasted on products that are either not valuable or not usable.

There are many reasons for bad products, and each topic in this book is intended to speak to some aspect of where these bad products come from, *but I have long argued that the root cause of wasted releases can most often be traced to poor definition of the role of the product manager in a company, and inadequate training of the people chosen for this role.*

This is a topic I've been thinking about for a long time—it is critically important because it gets to the core of what the job of the product manager truly needs to be.

As discussed earlier, the job of the product manager is to define—in detail—the product that the engineering team will build. In contrast, the role of product marketing is to tell the world about this product. These are extremely different jobs.

To be clear right from the start, I argue that every product needs a single, accountable product manager, who is responsible for the product definition (the combination of product requirements and user experience design that describe the product to be built). Unfortunately, when I begin working with a company, all too often I encounter one of three different situations:

Marketing-Driven Product: There is a product marketing or product manager-titled person responsible for market requirements, and then the product goes straight to engineering—bypassing detailed product requirements and the many tough decisions that are encountered through the discovery process (and also very often bypassing user experience design, but that's the subject of another topic).

Two People, One Role: The product definition role is split between a product marketing person responsible for "high-level" business requirements and a product manager person responsible for the "low-level" product requirements.

One Person, Two Roles: A product marketing person is asked to cover both roles (and the company sometimes calls these people product managers and sometimes product marketing).

Let's discuss each of these three situations and the problems they create:

Marketing-Driven Product

This situation is pretty easy to spot. The rest of the product team views this person as the marketing resource who might be useful for creating data sheets, training the sales force, and coming up with the naming and pricing, but in terms of defining the product, this person is largely discounted and ignored. There are plenty of Dilbert cartoons portraying this person, and we've all known this type of product manager.

While these people might be great at marketing, they are way over their heads when it comes to trying to discover and define in detail a valuable, usable and feasible product. In this situation, hopefully someone else on the product team—sometimes a lead engineer, sometimes an interaction designer, and sometimes a manager—steps in and performs the true product management function. If this person has the skills in addition to the bandwidth, the product may yet succeed. More often, however, the product is already in trouble right from the start.

My first exposure to product management was in this exact situation, and it initially kept me from wanting to have any association at all with this role. Fortunately, I met a guy that showed me what product management was really all about, and since that day I've worked to highlight the successful product managers and to redefine the role around these people.

Two People, One Role

This situation is also easy to spot, as there is no single person responsible for the product. A product marketing person (sometimes in this model called the "business owner" or the "business product manager") is responsible for the high-level product requirements, and a product manager (sometimes called a "technical product manager" or "product owner" in *Agile* teams) is responsible for the low-level product requirements.

The problem is that neither person truly owns the product and, more importantly, neither person feels nor behaves like they are ultimately responsible for the product. Further, this model is based on a flawed view of software that holds that you can define high-level requirements independent of detailed requirements and especially the user experience.

In companies with this model, product managers become little more than a spec-generation service. It is a frustrating job that tends to stifle innovation and rarely produces successful products.

Many larger companies with multiple business units evolve into these roles and then wonder why they can no longer come up with inspiring products that their customers love.

One Person, Two Roles

The problem with combining the product manager and product marketing roles into one position is that it is very hard to find someone who can do both types of jobs well. Each of these roles is critical for a product's success, and each requires special skills and talents. Creating a product is much different than telling the world about that product. I have known some truly exceptional people who can excel in both roles, but these people are very rare. As an organizational model, it just doesn't scale. Further, for all but the simplest of products, the role of the product manager as defined here is an all-consuming, full-time job, requiring a dedicated person. If you ask the product marketing person to cover the product management role, even if the person has the skills and talents required for both, it is unlikely he or she will have the bandwidth to do both jobs well.

This is most frequently a problem at enterprise software companies where supporting the sales force is a big job in itself, and there is a strong tendency for the product managers simply to pass along (perceived) requirements—from the big customers, to the sales reps, to the product managers, and then to the engineers. And—no surprise—this almost never results in valuable and usable products.

It is important to recognize that there are reasons for each of the organizational models described above, and I do understand that. But these companies are sacrificing far more than they realize. They are wasting entire product release cycles, and they are creating products that customers don't want, or must struggle with to use.

The Way Out

The way out of these situations is to clearly define the distinct roles of product manager and product marketing in your company. The product manager is responsible for defining—in detail—the product to be built, and validating that product with real customers and users. The product marketing person is responsible for telling the world about that product, including positioning, messaging and pricing, managing the product launch, providing tools for the sales channel to market and sell the product, and for leading key programs such as online marketing and influencer marketing programs.

Please note that while my personal focus is on product management, that focus should not be misconstrued as a belief that the product marketing role is unimportant. Quite the opposite. I have learned that it is important, and that great product marketing is extremely valuable. But it has little to do with the product manager role that I have described here.

In general, the product manager and product marketing person will communicate often and collaborate occasionally on specific topics, but there are two main interactions. First, the product marketing person will be *one of several key sources of input* to product requirements owned by the product manager. Second, the product manager will be one of the several key sources of input to marketing messages owned by product marketing.

Regardless of the title or organizational model, I promise you that behind every great product you will find an individual who is responsible for the definition of that product.

Remember: It doesn't matter how great your engineering organization is if the product manager doesn't give the engineers something valuable, usable and feasible to build.

Chapter 3:

PRODUCT MANAGEMENT VS. PROJECT MANAGEMENT

The Internet Changed This Too

In the previous chapter, I wrote about how important it is to clearly distinguish the roles of product management and product marketing. Many companies suffer from another related problem: when the roles of product management and project management are combined.

The reason so many Internet companies still define product management as including project management is because many of our practices came from the shipped software world. In the shipped software world (such as the *Office* software products from Microsoft became famous for), it is common to have product managers cover the project management role. However, while it might work for shipped software, this approach just doesn't migrate well to the Internet.

To understand why, first a little bit of Internet history. When Internet services came about, around 1996 or so, at first we struggled with whether to continue to call ourselves product managers, because things like a travel Web site seemed more service-oriented than a traditional shipped software product. But we quickly got over that.

We initially tried to continue having the product manager cover the project manager role. Early internet companies like Netscape and Yahoo! tried this approach but they ran into a problem: in the shipped software world, the product was generally packaged as a self-contained unit, with one release package serially following another often months or even years later. So the product generally was in the same granularity and frequency as the project, making it relatively easy for the product manager to double as the project manager. But in the Web services world, this model breaks down.

Most Internet service companies found that they needed to make more frequent, smaller releases to a larger common code base. And since a typical project required more work than a release interval (usually ranging from weekly to monthly), this quickly turns into parallel development and the *software train model* of releases. Most Internet companies beyond the startup phase use this train model.

The train model is really a topic unto itself. The most important point for this book is that a train requires active and strong project management which is not tied to specific projects, but rather to the release as a whole. A train typically contains features from many projects and product managers, and it has significant coordination requirements such as release management, engineering, site operations, customer service, and product management. Some Internet companies refer to the project manager of a release train as the train's *conductor*.

If you use the train model, and you have project managers dedicated to the release trains, you generally don't need product managers to cover project management too.

Back to the history lesson. As the release process at companies like Yahoo!, Netscape, AOL, and others became more sophisticated as the products and sites grew, the project management responsibilities were untangled from the product management role, and all of these companies developed very strong and dedicated project management competencies. Many newer Internet companies such as eBay and Google could not release the quantity and quality of software they do without their very strong project management team spanning product management, engineering and site operations.

Long story short, for Internet services companies, it is important that the roles be separate. You'll thrash in release management if you don't, and releases will consistently be delayed and take longer than they should.

If you are creating shipped software, I still think it's useful to separate the roles. This is more due to the nature of product management, which is all about discovering a product that is valuable, usable and feasible; versus project management, which is all about executing to deliver that product.

 What Makes A Great Project Manager?

Look at any successful company and you'll find a set of people who stand out and are the ones that really make the difference from other companies. It may be the difference between a great product or a terrible one. Or the difference between getting the business partnerships the company needs to reach its customers or getting lost in obscurity. Or the difference between getting the product out or having it stuck in perpetual delays.

eBay is by anyone's definition a very successful company, and it has some extremely strong people in each of these areas and more.

eBay has a very unusual product development process, but three key characteristics of this process stand out: it is extremely productive, extremely demanding, and it is a process predicated on an extremely strong project management competency.

The person that established this project management competency for eBay was Lynn Reedy, the very best project management mind I've ever had the privilege of working with. Before I joined eBay I thought I was pretty good at project management, but she showed me where the bar really was.

In some companies (much of Microsoft for example), the product manager is also responsible for running some or all of project management. I believe that developing strong project management skills is a big advantage for product managers. At the very least, your product will get to market faster, and—ultimately—it could make the difference between getting your product shipped at all. However, I also argue that the product manager and the project manager should be separate roles.

I think most people equate project management with *Microsoft Project*. But this is missing the real point of project management. Here are the seven skills that I think characterize great project managers like Lynn:

Sense of urgency. Just by walking into the room Lynn would instantly convey a sense of urgency. Pre-meeting banter was maybe 60 seconds, and then it was down to business. Partly this was due to her unique diet of sugar and caffeine, but in fact a sense of urgency–and efficiency—is at the heart of the eBay culture and was best personified by Lynn.

Framers. There are so many reasons for aimless, unconstructive meetings, but one of the biggest culprits is that it's not always clear to the participants exactly what the purpose of the meeting is, what problem is to be solved, and what the specific issues or obstacles are. Great project managers understand how to clearly and concisely identify and frame problems and run constructive meetings.

Clear thinking. The typical business issue generally includes multiple underlying causes with a healthy dose of politics, personal agendas and personalities thrown in. This results in a murky confusion that if left unaddressed, delays development progress. The project manager needs to isolate the separate issues, and untangle the emotion and baggage to expose the underlying problem and get everyone focused on pursuing the solution.

Data driven. Great project managers understand the key role that data plays in informing them about precisely where they are and where they need to go. They are constantly looking to improve the product development process and the result, and they know this begins with measurement. It is all too easy to just shoot from the hip—especially in time-sensitive situations—so it's essential for the project manager to insist on the data to make sure the decisions are made with the facts behind them.

Decisiveness. In most organizational models, the members of the product team don't actually report to the project manager, yet he or she must drive decisions. This is where the project manager must communicate the sense of urgency, clearly frame the problem, have rational and transparent reasoning, and make decisions based on the data. The project manager also needs to know when it is appropriate to collect data and recommendations from the team, and when to escalate issues to senior management.

Judgment. Much of the above hinges on good judgment—knowing when to push, when to escalate, when to get more information, and when to take someone aside and have a little private chat. This trait is harder to teach, but experience can help.

Attitude. Finally, there are always hundreds of very valid reasons why a product isn't ready to ship—not enough resources, not enough time, not enough money, etc. The job of the project manager is to get over each and every one of these obstacles. At their core, great project managers are great problem solvers. The great project manager doesn't make excuses, she makes it happen. She is tireless and unstoppable.

I truly believe that eBay would not be the success it is today without the project management discipline Lynn brought to the company and the culture.

Chapter 4:

PRODUCT MANAGEMENT VS. DESIGN

Understanding User Experience Design

Many product people complain to me that their company doesn't staff or even understand user experience design, and they know their product suffers for it. Most say that the UI engineers just do whatever they can and that, by default becomes the design. Sometimes it's the product managers who wade into the design waters and do whatever they can. And in other cases, companies try to outsource some visual design at the end of the product development process to add in pretty veneer just before the product goes into QA.

Others tell me that their company values good user experience design, but they don't really understand the roles or how a good design comes about.

This is a very serious problem that not enough companies are aware of.

It seems to me that the design community hasn't been doing enough to address this lack of recognition for their importance to a product. While they do a good job communicating among themselves (and there are some outstanding talents in the design community, including Mark Hurst, Hugh Dubberly, and Alan Cooper, to name a few), in general I think these guys spend a lot of time preaching to the choir. The message about the value they deliver is most needed by the teams without designers. One way to do this is to work on educating the wider product team about the need and benefits of designers to a product, especially the product managers.

The reason I care so much about this problem is simple. A good product requires a good user experience. And a good user experience requires the close collaboration of product management and user experience design.

This is a big topic, so let's start by getting on the same page in terms of what design includes. In this chapter I spell out what I consider the design-related roles essential to creating a good user experience. Note that I'm emphasizing roles rather than people, as it's possible to find people that can competently handle more than one role. But one way or the other you need these roles if you want a good user experience:

Interaction Design. These people are responsible for developing a deep understanding of the target users and coming up with the tasks, navigation, and flow that are both valuable and usable. Generally, the interaction designer maps product requirements to a design represented by wireframes, and passes them to the visual designer.

Visual Design. These people put the flesh on the wireframe and create the actual pages and user interface look and feel, which includes everything from the precise layout, colors, and fonts, but more importantly, the visual design communicates and evokes emotion in the product (which is far more important than you may think).

Rapid Prototyping. The prototypes work to capture the ideas of the product manager and designers into a prototype that can be tested on real users, and iterated upon.

Usability Testing. This person specializes in research and analysis of the users, evaluating whether products or prototypes allow a given user to easily achieve objectives. It includes recruiting appropriate test subjects, administering the tests, evaluating the results, and recommending alternatives.

The four design roles above work closely with the product manager to discover the blend of requirements and design that meet the needs of the user. The idea is to get to the point where the software is both *usable* (users can figure out how to use it) and *valuable* (users actually want to use it).

You will also need to ensure the software you're designing is *feasible*, so you need to have a software architect reviewing the progress and prototypes. More on this later.

For large products—especially at consumer Internet service companies—you really do need all four roles represented on your team. If you're an enterprise company and you'd like to differentiate your product from your competition, one of the easiest ways to do this is to create a good user experience. As a general rule, most enterprise products are very weak in this respect.

For smaller products, you may be able to double-up some of the roles. For example, I recently worked with a consumer Internet service startup in the Web 2.0 space which had assembled a terrific team of three: a product manager, an interaction designer (who also covered usability testing), and a visual designer (who also covered prototyping). This team of three worked extremely well together to quickly come up with numerous prototypes that they then tested with target users.

One other important note: Many companies realize they need to do something in this area, but they think they can outsource this user experience work to a design firm. To some degree you can, but beware that certain functions are more appropriate than others. For example, I don't recommend outsourcing the interaction designer role because of these three reasons:

1. It takes time, over the course of several projects, to truly develop the necessary understanding of users and customers. Most design contracts don't have the time to do that, and even if they do, that knowledge is lost when the next release comes up;

2. The interaction designer needs to be on hand and deeply involved all the way through the project, from the beginning to launch. Hundreds of detailed questions will come up during development and test—having an interaction designer there to make the right decisions immediately is critical;

3. The user experience of the product is simply too core to the company to not have in-house. Given the option, it's a better choice to outsource QA.

You can get away with outsourcing visual design, as there are a number of studios that can do what you need, especially if you have a strong interaction designer on staff. You can also outsource user research and/or usability testing, although it's often expensive and I'm a big fan of informal testing (see the chapter *Prototype Testing*). The product manager and interaction designer can often team up to cover this.

For the rapid prototyper, you can borrow a developer from your engineering team, as long as you make very clear to that person that this is completely different from production-level coding, and that he or she should not try to build a prototype where any of it can be reused later in the real product. In fact, they should consider all the code in a prototype as throw-away.

There's a great deal more to say on this critical topic than can be covered in this brief chapter, but hopefully this discussion lays the foundation. Which of these roles are currently covered within your product team and which ones are missing?

Chapter 5:

PRODUCT MANAGEMENT VS. ENGINEERING

Building The Right Product Versus Building The Product Right

If a great product is the result of combining a real customer need with a solution that's just now becoming possible, then it's easy to see why the relationship between the product manager and the engineering team is so critical.

The product manager is responsible for defining the solution, but the engineering team knows best what's possible, and they must ultimately deliver that solution. As a product manager, you'll quickly learn that if you have a good relationship with engineering, then the job can be a great one. If you don't, let's just say that you're in for some very long and frustrating days.

One key to this relationship is for each of you to understand that you are peers—neither position is subordinate to the other. As product manager, you are responsible for defining the right product, and your engineering counterpart is responsible for building the product right. You need both. You need to let your engineering counterpart do what he believes necessary to build a quality product, and he needs to give you the room to come up with a valuable and usable product.

Both sides can be a huge help to each other. Specifically, the engineers can be a big help to you as you work to discover a winning product. Remember that they generally know what's possible better than anyone else.

Here are three ways you can use your engineers to come up with a better product:

1. Get your engineers in front of users and customers. Not only will they learn a great deal from seeing users struggle first hand, but they will get a better appreciation for the issues and their severity. This is often the inspiration for much better ideas and solutions. You can jumpstart this easily by inviting an engineer along to your prototype testing.

2. Enlist the help of your engineers in exploring what's becoming possible as technology develops. Brainstorm the different technologies that are available or coming available, and how they might help solve the problems at hand.

3. Involve your engineers (or at least a lead engineer) or architect from the very beginning of the product discovery process to get very early assessments of relative costs of the different ideas, and to help identify better solutions. One of the most common mistakes that product managers make is to come up with a great product definition, and then throw it over the wall to engineering. That just postpones the critical negotiation process of what's wanted vs. what's possible until there's not enough time to be able to make good and informed decisions.

Similarly, you can actually be a big help to your engineers. Here are three ways you can help them do their job:

1. Keep the focus on *minimal* product. More on this later, but your job as product manager is not to define the ultimate product, it's to define the smallest possible product that will meet your goals. This point alone will fundamentally

improve the dynamic between product management and engineering.

2. Do everything you can to minimize *churn* once engineering begins to develop the product. Churn is changing requirements and product definition. Some churn will be unavoidable, and engineers understand that some things are beyond your control, but remember that this is not the time for trying out your latest-and-greatest ideas.

3. There will inevitably be questions that arise during implementation, including use cases that were missed or weren't completely thought through. This is normal, even in the best of product teams. However, your mission as the product manager during the implementation phase is to jump on their questions and get answers as fast as humanly possible, always keeping the focus on minimal product and minimizing churn.

With all this in mind, I always try to encourage the best engineers to come try their hand at product management. I remind them that it doesn't matter how great the engineering is if the team is not given something worthwhile to build. And I point out the many great products and companies that have been created by an engineer who knew what was possible and tackled the bigger question of what to build. It's great for their career development, and can be great for the product (and therefore the customers and the company).

How Do We Succeed With Remote Developers?

One of the most common situations today is where the product manager is in one location, and the engineering team is somewhere else. I don't only mean outsourcing to India, either. The remote development team might emerge from an acquisition or merger, or possibly your organization is large enough where the developers are located in a facility you are not.

When the developers are not sitting right next to you, then all of the normal challenges of communication and execution are magnified, often to the point where many teams get extremely frustrated with remote development, and some members openly challenge the benefits of the purported cost savings.

If you find yourself with a remote development team, there are three key things you can do to dramatically improve the odds of your success:

1. The farther away the team is from you—and the more the communication challenges of language, culture and time zones—the more pressure there is to ensure that you have done a very thorough job on the product spec. The nightmare project is where the product manager isn't sure what he wants built (or keeps changing his mind) and the remote engineering team is thrashing. It's like being on the wrong end of a whip—and a recipe for failure.

In the chapter *Reinventing the Product Spec*, I write about the importance of a high-fidelity prototype as the basis of the product spec. I won't repeat all the reasons for that here, but suffice it to say that if your team is remote, you absolutely want to make sure you use the high-fidelity prototype as your main communication mechanism—both for communicating the actual spec and for communicating changes. Written documents are hard enough to get people to read, but if it's written in a language that isn't native, and if the author isn't in the cube down the hall to clarify questions, you're asking for big trouble.

2. When a development team is local, resource conflicts (for example, two different managers give conflicting instructions) are typically caught and resolved quickly. With remote teams, you can expect lots of unpleasant surprises, and literally months can pass before the disconnects are identified. This is usually because the remote developers are forced to make assumptions about who wanted what and how to interpret the various instructions (and,

of course, the assumptions are not always correct). It is critical to have someone local manage all coordination with the remote team. This doesn't mean that all communication must be funneled through this person, but there should be no question to whom the engineering team is accountable. Sometimes this is a project manager and sometimes this is a director or VP of engineering who is based locally (near the product manager).

3. There are many good communication mechanisms available within most businesses today. In addition to e-mail and instant messaging, video conferencing technology is much improved, and VoIP has brought the costs way down for international calls. That said, there still is no substitute for establishing personal face-to-face relationships. At least once a quarter, the product manager should get out and spend some quality face time with the engineering team, meeting with the key architects and managers. These face-to-face visits will improve relationships and communication. Another great communication-building technique is to have an exchange program where key developers come stay with the product manager for a while.

With a talented remote team, and managing the relationship as I've described, you can actually come to enjoy this arrangement. Especially with engineers based in India, the time difference can make it such that every morning when you come in to work, you see progress waiting for you, and you can spend your day (and their night) reviewing, testing, and providing feedback. The result can be extremely fast cycle times.

Note that you can also have your prototyping resources in a remote location, but you'll have to work a little harder on the communication and be more flexible on your hours because of the very quick cycle times (several iterations a day).

Yet another solution to the problems of dealing with a remote development team involves locating the entire product team together in the remote location. I see this trend just starting, and I think it will grow. That said, you don't have to worry about this just yet. It has taken 10 years to develop the engineering and QA capabilities in these remote locations, and it'll likely take another 10 before these locations have skilled product managers and designers as well.

What About Outsourcing?

Just about every company I talk to now is outsourcing to one degree or another. Yet the results are decidedly mixed. I think there are several reasons for the problems that companies are having. Often the problems stem from issues with the product development process, or from language or cultural issues, but more often than not I think the core issue stems from using outsourcing for the wrong reasons.

If you're trying to create inspiring products, for most professional positions, outsourcing should *not* be about cost savings—it should be about assembling the right people for the product. Very often, you'll have to look beyond your immediate geographic vicinity for the best people. This might mean hiring someone that's based in another state, or in another country.

The sad truth about Silicon Valley is that it has become so expensive that many of the people you would like to hire can't afford to live here at the salary you can afford to pay them. Commuting only works to a degree. Eventually the talent supply runs out and you have to look elsewhere for the right team.

Fortunately, there are some terrific sources of outstanding product talent in places such as India, Eastern Europe (especially the Czech Republic, Hungary, Poland, and Slovakia), Northern Europe (especially the Netherlands, Sweden, and Germany), Israel, China, Singapore, Australia, and New Zealand. I know some amazing people in every one of these locations. One of the best teams I ever had the privilege to lead had members spread across Sweden, Silicon Valley, Boston, and India. We were building infrastructure that needed to support more than 20 million users and it's not at all clear we could have succeeded without the talents of the specific individuals involved.

One of my favorite companies is MySQL, which is a company that has embodied this philosophy for years. They are nominally based in Silicon Valley and Sweden, but their product team and even their executives are scattered all over the globe. They are a true virtual organization, and they are able to benefit from some of the very best database and system software talent to be found anywhere. It is not easy for them to manage a completely distributed product team, but I'd argue that very likely they would not have been able to accomplish what they have if they had picked a single location on the globe, and tried to be a typical centralized company.

Just as manufacturing jobs were forced out of Silicon Valley in the '80s, several other types of jobs are moving out today—

especially customer service, QA, and to a somewhat lesser extent, engineering. It's becoming common to have the architects and QA managers located at the company's headquarters, along with product management and design, and then to have the rest of the team at locations either together or dispersed around the globe.

The key is to realize that it's all about the team and the caliber of the individuals it consists of. Many managers don't quite get this, and they are stunned to learn that there can be as much as a 20X difference in productivity among their staff in the same job class. Which will do better—the team that has five very strong people chosen for their proven skills, or the team of 15 that was hired or assembled based on their location? This productivity factor can easily dwarf perceived financial savings. Similarly, it can turn a top engineer living in the very expensive city of Stockholm into a bargain.

There are additional factors that come into play, but it's my firm belief that everything begins with the right product team, and if your product team decides you need to outsource, I hope you do it for the right reasons—to get the right people for your product team and not just because you think you'll save a few bucks.

Engineering Wants To Rewrite!?!

Few words are more dreaded by product managers than being told by engineering: "No more new features! We need to stop and rewrite! Our code base is a mess, it can't keep up with the number of users, it's a house of cards, we can no longer maintain it or keep it running!"

This situation has happened to many companies in the past, and continues to happen today. It happened to eBay in 1999, and the company came far closer to collapsing than most people ever realized. It happened to Friendster a few years ago, opening the door for MySpace to take over social networking. It happened to Netscape during the browser wars with Microsoft, and everyone knows who won. The truth is that most companies never recover.

When a company does get into this situation, the company typically blames engineering. But in my experience, the harsh truth is that it's usually the fault of product management. The reason is that when this comes up, it's usually because for several years, product managers have been pounding the engineering organization to deliver as many features as the engineering team possibly can produce. The result is that at some point, if you neglect the infrastructure, all software will reach the point where it can no longer support the functionality it needs to.

During this rewrite, you're forced to stop forward progress for what the customers see. You might think that the rewrite will take only a few months (more about that below), but invariably it takes far longer, and you are forced to stand by and watch your customers leave you for your competitors, who in the meantime, are continuing to improve their product.

If you haven't yet reached this situation, here's what you need to do to make sure you never do—you need to allocate a percentage of your engineering capacity to what at eBay we called "headroom." Since many of the issues you run into with rapid growth have to do with scale, the idea behind headroom is to avoid slamming into ceilings. You do this by creating room for growth in the user base, growth in transactions, and growth in functionality; essentially, keep the product's infrastructure able to meet the organization's needs.

The deal with engineering goes like this: Product management takes 20% of the team's capacity right off the top and gives this to engineering to spend as they see fit. They might use it to rewrite, re-architect, or re-factor problematic parts of the code base, or to swap out database management systems, improve system performance—whatever they believe is necessary to avoid ever having to come to the team and say, "we need to stop and rewrite."

If you're in really bad shape today, you might need to make this 30% or even more of the resources. However, I get nervous when I find teams that think they can get away with much less than 20%.

If you are currently in this situation, the truth is that your company may not survive. But if you are to have a chance of pulling through, here's what you'll need to do:

Step 1: Do a realistic schedule and timeline for making the necessary changes that engineering identifies. Most of the time in a normal development project, an experienced engineering team will come up with fairly accurate estimates. The exception to this rule is this case of rewrites—here the estimates are often wildly optimistic—largely because few teams have any real experience with true rewrites. You must make informed decisions in this situation, so you'll have to go through every line item on the schedule to make sure that the dates are realistic.

Step 2: If there's any way humanly possible to break up the rewrite into chunks to be done incrementally with user-visible product development continuing on the site, you should absolutely do so. Even though the rewrite might now stretch over two years instead of nine months, if you can find a way to continue to make forward progress on user-visible functionality—even if it's only with 25% to 50% of the capacity—this is incredibly important for the product to stay relevant in the marketplace, particularly in the fast-paced Internet space.

Step 3: Since you'll only have very limited ability to deliver user-visible functionality, you will need to pick the right features, and make sure you define them right.

After eBay's near-death experience, the team made sure they wouldn't put the company at risk again. This meant immediately beginning another rewrite, this time well in advance of issues. In fact, due to their very rapid growth, eBay ended up rewriting a third time, this time translating the entire site into a different programming language and architecture. And they did this massive, multi-million-line rewrite over several years while at the same time managing to deliver record amounts of new functionality and—most importantly—without impacting the user base. It's the most impressive example of rebuilding the engine in mid-flight that I know of.

The best strategy for dealing with this situation is to not get to this point. You need to pay your taxes and remember to dedicate at least 20% to headroom. If you haven't had this discussion with your engineering counterpart, do so today.

Chapter 6:

RECRUITING PRODUCT MANAGERS

Finding Great Product Managers

Probably the single most common question I get from CEOs is this: Where can I find great product managers?

I tell them that often the great product managers they're looking for are already in their organization, hiding under a different title— maybe a software engineer, user experience designer, or a Systems Engineer (SE), just waiting to be discovered. But whether you recruit product managers from inside or outside, the easiest way to spot them is to have a clear understanding of the characteristics to look for. So in this chapter I'll enumerate the specific traits and skills you're looking for.

Personal Traits and Attitude

Most skills can be learned, however, there are some traits that are very difficult to teach, and as such they should form the foundation of any search for a product manager.

Product Passion

There are some people out there who just love products—they live, eat, and breathe them. Great product managers have a love and respect for good products, no matter where they come from, and they live to create them.

This passion for product is an essential ingredient as it will often be called upon to provide the motivation to get through the many very difficult challenges—and long hours—of defining a great product. Further, the product manager will need to inspire the rest of the product team, and the passion for a product is contagious.

It is fairly easy to determine whether or not you are talking to such a person by simply asking them what some of their favorite products are and why. It is hard to feign passion—the insincerity comes through loud and clear. Ask for examples from different domains. Ask what they would improve on their favorite product if they were the product manager. Ask about bad products too.

Customer Empathy

The ideal product manager does not necessarily have to come from your target market (there are pros and cons to this), but they absolutely need to be able to empathize with your target market. This trait is often difficult to find in high-technology companies trying to produce mass-market products. We tend to want to think of our users as we think of ourselves and our friends. However, the target market very likely has quite different values, priorities, perceptions, tolerances, experiences, and technical understandings.

Ask the candidates about the target market and how they believe they might be different from themselves. Try and detect how the candidate feels about the target market and, most importantly, does the candidate respect and empathize with that target market? Or does he view his job as "enlightening" the target market?

This is doubly important for international products, or those products targeted at specific countries or cultures. There are many similarities and, more importantly, many differences between cultures. Many of the differences are incidental and not important to defining products. However, some of the differences are essential. Does the candidate you are talking to have enough understanding of the target market to know which is which?

Intelligence

There is really no substitute for innate intelligence. Product management is about insights and judgment, both of which require a sharp mind. Hard work is also necessary, but for this job, it is not sufficient.

Hiring very smart people is harder than it sounds. Much depends on the strength and security of the hiring manager. You've probably heard the old adage about A's hiring A's, and B's hiring C's. It's true. Hiring smart people speaks to the company culture which is another important topic in its own right, but suffice it to say here that if your goal is a truly great product, it is simply not going to happen if you can't find a truly bright product manager.

Assuming you are anxious to find the brightest, most insightful person possible, one technique is to drill your candidates on their ability to problem solve. Microsoft is famous for their very intensive and effective interviewing for intelligence based on problem solving. The technique is to use one or more experts in some topic to drill the candidate on a problem. The interviewer is not looking so much at whether or not the candidate simply knows the right answer (knowledge rather than intelligence), but rather, how well they deal with not knowing the answer. How does the candidate work out problems? What is the thought process? When the candidate comes up with a solution, the interviewer changes the question somewhat and asks what the candidate would do then. This is done continuously until the candidate is eventually forced to deal with a scenario he or she doesn't know the answer to. Then the candidate is asked to verbalize how he or she would go about solving that problem. With practice, this can be a very effective technique in assessing a candidate's problem solving capability.

Another approach is to ask two or three people in your organization who are well known for their intellectual prowess, to interview this person, and help you determine the candidate's problem-solving ability.

Work Ethic

Not every role in the product team requires the same level of commitment and effort. However, the product manager role is not for someone who is afraid of hard work. It comes along with the responsibility; the product manager is the person ultimately held accountable for the success of the product, and this burden weighs heavily on the successful product manager.

Even when skills such as time management and the techniques of product management are mastered, the successful product manager is still consumed with the product. Can you have a family and a non-work life and be a successful product manager? I believe you can. At least once you have some experience. But there are many people that want to be able to work 40 hours a week and—most importantly—leave their work problems at the office when they go home at the end of the day. This unfortunately is not the life of a successful product manager.

I believe in being very frank with new candidate product managers about the level of effort required for successful product management. It is not about requiring the product manager to work certain hours. If you have to actually ask or tell the product manager to come in to work during a critical point or otherwise point out to them that their presence is needed in the office, you have the wrong person for the job.

Keep in mind that the level of effort and commitment is not uniform throughout the lifecycle of the project. There are certain phases that are much more intense than others. What won't change for the successful product manager is the degree to which they care and worry about their product and the lengths they are willing to go to ensure its success.

Integrity

Of all the members of the product team, the product manager most needs to reflect the values of the company and the product. In most organizational structures, the product manager does not directly manage the people on the project team, and as such, he can't simply direct the people to do his bidding. Rather, he must work by influencing those on his team. This persuasion is done by mutual trust and respect—both of which depend on the integrity of your product manager.

Trust and respect is built over time by the successful product manager demonstrating the traits and skills of a strong product team leader. If the product manager is not perceived to have integrity, or honesty, or fairness when dealing with his teammates, then the product manager will not have the degree of collaboration and team effectiveness that he needs to get the job done well.

The product manager may not be an expert in every role of the product team, but he should have a deep understanding and respect for what each team member is responsible for, and he should be willing to trust those people to do their job.

As the main interface between the product team and both the executive team and the sales organization, the product manager is often put in difficult situations, such as being asked to deliver products earlier, or with special features for large customers. The product team will watch closely how the product manager handles these situations.

As with intelligence, assessing someone's integrity can be difficult—especially outside candidates who are unknown to your organization. For candidates with previous experience as product managers, you can ask them about how they dealt with the stresses in past products. Press for details of particular situations; what made the situation hard and how was it dealt with?

Confidence

Many people think of confidence as a result of experience. However, while experience may help build confidence, many very experienced product managers simply do not project confidence. At the same time, you can sometimes find brand-new college graduates simply bursting with confidence (although this is generally the confidence that comes from not yet knowing what they're in for).

Confidence is an important trait because the entire product team, executive team, and sales organization is looking to the product manager to convince them that what they are investing their time and money and careers in will be successful, and that the vision is a good one. In communicating persuasively, confidence is a critical ingredient, and people are more likely to follow a leader who has it, rather than one who does not.

Attitude

The successful product manager sees himself as the CEO of the product. He takes full responsibility for the product, and does not make excuses. The successful product manager knows he is ultimately responsible for the success of the product. More importantly, he knows there are many very valid reasons for the product not to ship, or fail in the market when it does—the product is too difficult to build, it will take too long to get to market, it will cost too much, it will be too complicated, etc. But he knows it is his job to see that each and every one of these obstacles is overcome.

This does not mean that he micromanages the product team, or that he tries to do it all himself, but rather that he is quick to take the blame if something goes wrong, and equally quick to give credit to the rest of the team when it goes well. The successful product manager knows that it is through the rest of the team that his product vision will become a reality, but that it is his product vision they are building.

Skills

In order to succeed at the job of product management, there are several skills that are important. If the person has the right personal traits, I believe all these skills can be learned.

Applying Technology

One reason so many successful product managers come from the engineering ranks is that a big part of defining a successful product is in understanding new technology and seeing how it might be applied to help solve a relevant problem.

While you don't need to be able to invent or implement the new technology yourself in order to be a strong product manager, you do need to be comfortable enough with the technology that you can understand it and see its potential applications.

There are many ways to develop this skill. Taking classes, reading books and articles, and talking with engineers and architects can help you learn. Ask the senior engineers on your product team their recommendations for ways to learn more about the technological possibilities. Brainstorming sessions with the engineering team are another way to learn how new technologies might be applied.

Focus

As the saying goes, "The main thing is to keep the main thing the main thing." There are so many distractions out there, especially for the product manager trying to create a product that customers will love. The ability to keep the focus on the key problem to be solved at any given moment, and not succumb to creeping featurism, or the loud voices of a few key people or customers, requires tremendous discipline—both company discipline and personal discipline.

The truth is that nearly every product has features that are not really all that important—if the features were never there, it would not significantly impact the sales or customer satisfaction. Much more often, if the features were not there, the product would be better for it as more users could comprehend and appreciate the resulting simpler product. Focus will help you reduce the number of cluttering features, reduce the time it takes you to build the product, and therefore the time it takes you to get to market and your costs of getting it there.

Time Management

In today's e-mail, instant message, and mobile phone-based world where distractions abound, it is so very easy to come in to work early in the morning, work frantically all day—even skipping food—and then head home late into the night, not having actually accomplished anything important for your product. This is because you have spent the day chasing fires and working on "urgent" items.

It is absolutely essential to get very skilled at quickly distinguishing that which is important from that which is urgent, and learn to prioritize and plan your time appropriately. If you can't manage to get the time to focus on those tasks which are truly important to your product, your product will fail.

I have known too many product managers who burn themselves out with 70-hour workweeks, but the worst part is when I tell them that they're not actually doing their job. The natural response is that they just don't have any more time and can't work any harder. I then go into my lecture on time management and working smarter. Rather than feel like they need to attend every meeting or be constantly available on e-mail, they need to spend their time on the activities that will actually make a difference. So much of what these people spend time doing is avoidable.

Communication Skills

While communication skills can, for the most part, be learned, it can take years to become an effective speaker or writer, and these skills will be required from the start. As discussed above, the product manager influences others by persuasion rather than authority— making his case by communicating either through writing, speaking or both.

Speaking skills can be partially assessed during the interview itself, but written skills should be assessed specifically. I like to suggest that product manager candidates bring in examples of written material such as nonproprietary white papers or strategic documents.

While good communication skills are absolutely essential, it is important to emphasize that speaking with an accent, or minor grammatical issues with a non-native language, do not constitute poor communication skills. The person must speak clearly enough to be easily understood, and write powerfully enough to persuade, but perfect pronunciation or grammar are not required.

Product managers spend a great deal of time writing—composing e-mails, specs, white papers, strategy papers, data sheets, competitive product reviews, and more. The successful product manager only takes the time to write these documents if he believes people are going to read them. And since they are going to be read, they need to do their job well, which is typically to describe, educate and/or persuade.

Being able to write clear and concise prose is a skill that product managers use every day. The successful product manager realizes that the readers are constantly evaluating him based on his writings. Especially with senior management, sometimes these writings are all they have to go on.

The other major form of communication that product managers frequently need to employ is giving a presentation. Presenting in front of a group—particularly a large group—is hard for many people. Presenting effectively is even harder. Yet this is an important skill for a product manager since many of the most important events in the life of a product require the product manager to stand up in front of a group of company executives, major customers or the company sales force and—in the short time he or she has—explain what the product is about and why it is important.

We have all sat through terrible presentations—with slide after endless slide, the speaker simply reading the bullets, people straining to read the too-small print, meaningless graphics, and being unclear what the key messages are and why you should care. Not only are these presentations ineffective at conveying the purpose to the team, they are also a waste of time.

In contrast, the successful product manager has a minimal number of slides, he is engaging, clearly knowledgeable and passionate about his product, he speaks clearly and to the point, his slides provide relevant supporting data for what he is saying, and he has unambiguously stated his main points and what he needs from the audience after the presentation. His presentation finishes on time (or even early), he entertains questions and, if he can't provide a clear, useful answer immediately, he follows up diligently and promptly with the questioner and, if appropriate, the entire audience. The book *Presenting to Win: The Art of Telling Your Story* by Jerry Weissman is a good guide to improving your presentation skills.

Business Skills

Finally, business skills are also important for the product manager. As the main interface with the rest of the company, the product manager will need to work with company finance staff, marketing people, sales, and executive management—using the language and concepts that these people deal with.

I sometimes talk of product managers needing to be bilingual. Not in Chinese and English. They need to be able to converse equally well with engineers about technology as they do with executives and marketers about cost structures, margins, market share, positioning, and brand.

This is one reason why so many product managers are recruited out of business school. The product organization knows that they need someone who can talk the language of the business side, so they hire an MBA. I have known some great product managers that have come through the MBA path, but business skills are but one part of the mix required for a successful product manger, and they can certainly be learned in places other than business schools. It is at least as common that an engineer moves into product management and acquires the business skills required by reading books, taking courses, and getting coaching and assistance from mentors in the finance and marketing organizations.

So where do you find these people?

After reading this list of traits and skills, you may be thinking that such people are extremely rare. They are rare—about as rare as good products. But few hires you make will be as critical as your product managers, so it is worthwhile to interview for these characteristics and set the bar high.

There are different schools of thought on recruiting product managers. Many companies think that all you need is someone from the marketing organization or someone with an MBA. In the old-school definition of product manager, this may have been true, but today this is a recipe for failure.

Many companies prefer MBAs from top business schools who have a technical undergraduate degree combined with applicable industry experience. This can work well if you keep in mind that a consistent problem with MBA programs—even from the top-tier schools—is that they almost never teach product management, so it is dangerous to assume that the recent MBA grad has any idea how to be a product manager.

My favorite source for product managers is to look for people with the characteristics described above and then use training, an informal mentoring program, and/or a formal employee development program to develop these people into strong product managers. Such people might be found virtually anywhere in the company. I've seen outstanding product managers come out of engineering, user experience design, customer service, professional services, product marketing, sales, and the user community. Often these people will approach management asking how they can get more involved in the product. It can also be useful for senior management to approach top performers from across the company about the possibility of product management, as this can be essential experience for those on an executive track.

 How Important Is Domain Experience?

Recently a friend called to ask my opinion of a product management leader job candidate—I'll call him David—with whom I've worked in the past. The hiring manager is an exec at a large consumer Internet services company. He really liked David, but his question to me was: "He's clearly an expert at enterprise software, but could he succeed at our type of business?"

I had to laugh, and I went on to explain that just over four years ago I got a similar call about David. His future manager asked me, "Clearly the guy was great at infrastructure software, but could he handle enterprise software?"

In truth, David is not an infrastructure guy, or an enterprise guy, or a consumer services guy. His education wasn't even in technology—he studied finance. He is, however, one very smart guy, and one of the best product managers I know. One of the things that David does extremely well is that he can tackle new domains and new technologies very quickly, and this has allowed him to excel with several very different types of products in different domains and industries.

I'm often asked about the need for applicable domain or industry expertise for product managers. Many product managers are, in fact, hired exclusively for their domain experience, and I do think there are a few products where domain expertise is truly essential. If I ever need a defibrillator one day, I hope there was a product manager on the team that designed it that knew something about cardiac care. But in my experience, this is by far the exception rather than the rule.

I'll go even further. It can be dangerous for a product manager to have too much domain expertise. I say that because people that have spent a long time building their mastery of one domain often fall into another common product management trap: they believe they can speak for the target customer, and that they are more like their target customer than they really are. The product manager needs to constantly revisit assumptions about the domain and the customers. It's not impossible for people with deep domain expertise to do this, but they have to work harder at it to remain open-minded to new developments and options.

This is not to say that you don't need domain expertise in order to do a good job with your product—in fact I think understanding your product domain is absolutely essential, and I don't mean superficial knowledge either. But I believe that strong product managers can come up to speed on most new product domains very quickly if they approach the education process aggressively. I've learned that it generally takes me one to three months to come up to speed on a domain I haven't worked on before, to the point where I feel confident charting a product strategy. Some people can probably learn faster, and others might take a little longer.

I also believe that there are some different skills required for leading enterprise products, versus infrastructure, versus consumer services versus consumer electronics. For example, if your product is sold to a relatively small number of large enterprises (as opposed to hundreds of thousands or millions of consumers), then some different techniques are used to understand requirements and try out product ideas. It is also important to understand the different types of sales and distribution channels because these impact the product as well. If hardware is involved, you need to understand the process and time-line differences. For large-scale consumer services, the issues of scale and community management can destroy you if you don't know how to manage them.

Overall, I consider about 80% of the skills and talents of a product manager to be applicable across the different types of products.

This is also not a statement against the value of experience in general, but I have found that the most valuable experience is not what you learn about some product domain or technology (that is probably obsolete now anyway), but rather what you've learned about the process of creating great products, leading a product team, and managing growth. It's also what you've learned about yourself and how to improve the next time.

Very related to domain expertise is the topic of technology expertise. This used to come up more frequently than it does now, but I still hear it. I saw a job description the other day for an enterprise application company looking for a product manager with direct experience creating *Linux*-based products. While it's true that there are some important differences between operating systems, if the product manager can't very quickly assess the important points as it impacts his or her product, then this person has much greater issues than just lacking *Linux* expertise.

With high-tech products, it's all about how quickly you can learn new technologies and, more importantly, envision how you can apply the new technology to the problems you are trying to solve.

Technologies change so fast that product managers must be skilled at quickly learning new technologies and solving problems in new domains. When I interview prospective product managers, I'm looking not to see exactly what they already know, but for each of their products, what did they need to learn, how long did it take them, and how did they apply that knowledge?

 ## Does Age Matter?

If you have been wondering what's going on with all these startups with 20-something-year-old founders and product leaders, you're not alone. There are some great companies that have been started by some very young people, several of whom dropped out of college to pursue their ideas. While experience can be extremely valuable, there is a serious problem with people discounting product leaders because of their youth.

In truth, there are outstanding product leaders across the age spectrum. But how is it that someone can be just 25 years old and already an exceptional product leader? First, remember that the Internet has only been used by the widespread public since 1995 or so, so anyone who today is 25 or older probably has the same amount of experience online as the rest of us do. And people who were in their teens during the rise of the Internet grew up taking for granted technologies that many are still trying to figure out. Further, while experience can play an important role and naturally develops over time, other traits such as innate intelligence and product passion are not a function of age.

I personally had to get used to the idea of working for someone in their early 20s when I worked for Marc Andreessen, the young co-founder of Netscape. But I quickly forgot about how old he was once I started seeing how quickly he absorbed new technologies and assimilated the literally hundreds of customer visits he was doing at the time. Anyone just listening to him would assume he was at least in his 40s, based on his command of the business.

But what this is really all about is finding great product people—regardless of their age, gender or race. I'm not here to talk about the moral issues involved in the different forms of discrimination, but I do want to talk about the business issues. I believe there are still stereotypes and biases that get in the way of companies creating the best product teams and products possible.

One reason I love Silicon Valley so much is because the people here are so diverse. But even in the most progressive of companies, I think there are often hiring biases based on our mental image of a great product leader. For example, we know that communication skills are essential for a strong product manager, so we sometimes look for someone with native English-language skills, even though others who may be much stronger candidates have more than passable language skills.

I point this out not to chastise anyone but just to raise awareness that some truly outstanding product leaders may be overlooked by unintentionally restricting our view of what makes a great product manager and where great product ideas come from. So the next time that 22-year-old college hire comes to you with a product idea, you may want to listen. Her idea might be the next Facebook.

Chapter 7:

MANAGING PRODUCT MANAGERS

Building The Team That Will Build Your Company

I have long advocated setting the bar high for your product managers. These people are absolutely essential to the success of your products, and hence your business. Yet, when I speak with managers of product management, they often explain that they have inherited an organization where many of the people with "product manager" titles were really product marketing people. These so-called product managers had all the problems I described in earlier chapters, and they were struggling with how to correct the situation.

So here I'd like to discuss the role and responsibilities of those that manage product managers.

Typically this individual is given the title Director or VP of Product Management. This job is among the most important positions in any high-tech company. Few positions will have more impact on the future success of the company than the head of product management. A successful product can literally redefine the course of the business, while a failed product can sink it. As a result, this job is usually characterized by massive success or massive failure—and little in between.

These people have two essential responsibilities. First, they must build a strong team of product managers. Second, they are responsible for the company's overall product strategy and the various products in the company's portfolio. I'll discuss each of these responsibilities in turn.

Building the Product Management Team

It is the primary job of every manager to build and develop the capabilities of his or her team, but this is especially crucial for the role of Director of Product Management because of the high-impact nature of the product management position. An inadequate product manager is almost certain to fail, resulting in wasted product cycles, frustrated users, and lost customers. For many positions in the company, the truth is that you can often get away with sub-par employees because there are others who will pick up the slack. However, given that most products just have a single product manager for this position, this is rarely the case. Your only real hope if the product manager isn't fully capable is that someone else on the product team—perhaps a lead engineer—steps up to do what's necessary.

If you find yourself managing a team of product managers where some are not up to the task, then you have to correct the situation immediately. Some people will just never be successful product managers—they just aren't a fit for the position's demands and no amount of training or coaching is going to change that. However, I've found that for many product managers, you can in fact significantly improve their performance. I don't want this to sound self-serving since it is no secret that I spend a good deal of my time helping companies develop the skills of their product managers, but one way or another the product management leader needs to ensure that every team member is up to speed.

I believe that every new product manager needs roughly three months of hard learning before you can entrust them with the responsibility of guiding a product. During this time, the new product manager needs to immerse herself with target users and customers, get educated on the relevant technologies, and study the market and competitive landscape. Throughout the process, the manager should be facilitating and overseeing the learning curve. Note that this already assumes the product manager understands the actual skills and responsibilities of a product manager. These three months apply even to experienced product managers. They still need to learn about your unique customers and domain.

When you hire a new product manager to the team, establish a program so that he or she can get the needed exposure to users and technologies. For those product managers that you already have and are already in the midst of managing their products, if they're behind on understanding the users, then you will want to make sure that they start a program like this in parallel with their other responsibilities. But make sure they clearly understand their need to get up to speed.

If you determine that the product manager is unable or unwilling to do what is necessary to execute their duties at any level, it is your job as the manager to find someone that is. To anyone that has ever had to remove someone, you know this is no fun. But this is one reason for your higher pay, and you owe it to the rest of your team, company, and customers to correct the situation. Do everything you can to help the person find a job they can succeed at, but keep your focus laser sharp on getting the right people in place who can do the job that is necessary.

Once you are convinced that the members of your team are capable of success and properly equipped to succeed, then you will need to step back and let these talented people do their job. If you micro-manage your product managers, they will not step up and take ownership the way you need them to. If you can't trust your product managers, you need to find product managers you can trust. This doesn't mean you shouldn't ask questions and be constantly available to help—you absolutely should. But if you empower strong people and let them do their jobs, I promise you that you'll be amazed at what they can do.

Note that you've first got to make sure you have strong people before you empower them. If you empower people who aren't capable, you are abdicating your responsibility as manager. And if you micromanage people who are not capable, you are essentially doing their job for them.

Every good manager knows that the best way to look good is for the members of his or her team to look good. As such, always hire people that you believe are smarter than yourself, and then do everything you can to help them succeed.

Defining the Company's Product Strategy

Nobody is more responsible or more accountable for the suite of products a company offers than the head of the product management organization. This person decides what products to pursue, and then closely reviews the strategy and progress for each product.

The head of product management must have a deep and current understanding of the company's business strategy so that she can ensure the product strategy directly supports the business strategy. This individual also takes the leadership role in defining the product vision and working with the product managers on the team to deliver on this vision. The product principles (see the chapter *Product Principles*) are typically established by the full product management team, but the head of product management leads this effort and ensures that the products adhere to these principles as much as possible.

Even with the best team of product managers, each doing an outstanding job, you will still have cross-product conflicts as each product manager works to optimize his own product. The head of product management must work to identify and resolve these cross-product issues.

Similarly, the head of product management is responsible for the portfolio roadmap—taking an overall look at the many product releases that are planned, and considering the business needs and customer impact.

Finally, the head of product management will need to manage executive relationships within the organization. It is essential that all of the key players in the company—particularly the CEO—have a good and trusting relationship with the head of product management. The entire company depends on this person, and he must be open and transparent with his decisions and reasons, accessible and approachable by all. She must be receptive to new ideas from any source, but also respected enough that she can push back when appropriate on conflicting or vacillating priorities.

As you can see, this is an extremely demanding job, but great product companies have great people in this role, and this is no coincidence.

 How Do We Meaure Product Managers?

Very often I'm asked how product managers should be measured. I have long believed that the only true measure of the product manager is the success of his or her product. While I still believe that, it's not a very satisfying answer, as it's not clear what is the best way to measure a product's success. Is it revenue? Profit? The number of users? Page views? All of these indicators can be useful, but they don't really provide the big picture needed for a true measurement of a product manager's success.

Recently, a new business metric has been gaining traction across a number of different industries: Net Promoter Score (NPS). It's a very simple metric, and you can read all about it at www.netpromoter.com.

Here's how it works: You ask your customers how likely they would be to recommend your product to others, on a scale of 0-10. Those who rate 9 or 10 are considered "promoters" (they're out there telling their friends how much they love your product, and are actively evangelizing for you); those who rate 7-8 are lukewarm or neutral; and those who rate 0-6, the "detractors," that is, they not only won't recommend your product, they may even actively warn their friends or the public against your product. If you take the percentage of promoters and subtract the percentage of detractors, you get the NPS, which essentially tells you if you have more people cheering for you or against you.

Quite a few companies already track this metric, and those that rate very highly won't surprise you—companies like Apple, Amazon, Google and eBay.

I like this metric a lot because it puts the focus on the product and the overall customer experience. If, as we like to say in this business, it's all about creating happy customers, then this is a measure of exactly that. Yes, in theory you could have 100% very happy customers, but you end up going out of business because you're losing money on every customer. But for a single metric, I believe this keeps the focus of the company on creating happy customers, which is what fuels growth. And in terms of profitability, the most cost-effective sales or marketing program is your own customers doing the sales and marketing work for you. A great product with happy customers lowers these other (often very significant) costs, which contributes to profitability.

Another benefit of this metric is that it leads to the concept of good revenue and bad revenue. For example, let's say the company is approached by a big potential sponsorship or advertising partner that covets your user base and believes they can effectively sell their product on your site. This could be a good thing or a bad thing, depending on how it's done.

If it's done poorly, the short-term revenue might be nice, but if it hurts your customer experience, this will be reflected in the NPS, and your business growth will be slowed. On the other hand, if it's done well—for example, by working collaboratively with the advertising partner—it could be either neutral to the customer experience or even contribute to the experience. This will help your business grow more quickly.

This is why specials (doing explicitly-defined work for a specific customer typically in exchange for their agreement to purchase your product) are so dangerous. They represent bad revenue, and hurt your company's ability to deliver products that create happy users.

You can compare your NPS across companies and even across industries, which is interesting, but NPS is most useful as a way to measure your own progress towards improving your products and services. So if you don't already measure your NPS, consider doing so as soon as possible. Then you can start watching how the changes you make to your products impact the score. Make sure you're always moving in the right direction, and consider the impact on the NPS of everything you do.

Where Should Product Management Live?

Many companies struggle with where product management should live in the organization. The choices for most companies are most often engineering or marketing. If you have the right personalities, it can work in either place, but I'm actually not a fan of it residing in either.

The most common situation I find in the companies I work with is that product management lives within the marketing organization. The problem with this organizational design is that it is based on the misconception that you get products from talking to your customers, and that it is marketing's job to talk to customers. I won't repeat all the fallacies of this line of thinking here, but suffice it to say that there are several key reasons why you won't find successful products just by asking your customers. Also problematic is the fact that what usually happens is that the product marketing role and the product management role get combined within the marketing organization. These roles—and the skills required to execute them well—are so different that what usually ends up happening is that one or the other (or both) gets poorly executed.

The next most common situation I encounter is that product management is put in the engineering organization. While this has the benefit of putting the people who invent and design the product next to the people who actually build the product, this can also be problematic. Why? Because engineering organizations are typically designed to focus on building a product right, rather than building the right product. It's easy for the product management team to be consumed in the details and pressures of producing detailed specs rather than looking at the market opportunity and discovering a winning product strategy and roadmap. It takes a different mindset and different skills to come up with the right product to build. Moreover, engineering is essentially an execution-based activity, and it can be hard to perform discovery activities in an organization optimized for execution.

So if not the marketing organization, and if not the engineering organization, then where?

I am a big believer in raising the level of the product organization to be organizationally on par with engineering and marketing. Ideally, the product organization includes the design team, because the interaction between product management and user experience design absolutely needs to be as close as possible. Increasingly, you'll see an organization with the name of Product or Product Management or Product Management and Design— often with a VP of Product or even a Chief Product Officer running it.

There are several benefits to this organizational design, but the biggest reason is that the head of product needs to have a seat at the table on the executive team. Companies are all about products, and marketing and engineering are each critical components with their own considerations and challenges, and it's easy for the product to get lost in these issues. Additionally, this organizational structure makes it clear that the product is not being driven by the technology, and not being driven solely by the sales or marketing needs either.

One special case exists in many larger companies. Often large companies have a centralized engineering function and decentralized business units. This lets the company focus on multiple business lines, while potentially enjoying efficiencies in common engineering services. In such organizations, the product management and design function might be located in the centralized engineering/product development organization, or it might be in its own organization, or it might be a part of the business units themselves. Often in such an organization, the business unit managers must play a major product management role, creating problems if the product management team isn't part of the business unit. In these situations, I usually prefer integrating product management and design into the business units.

While I've explained my reasons for the ideal locations, it can be very hard to implement organizational structural change, and your company may not be willing or able to go this route. This does not necessarily mean that you're destined for problems. It still boils down to the people involved and the skills they bring. If you can develop your product team's skills and demonstrate their value across the company, any of these organizational structures can succeed.

 Examples

You can see example product strategies, product roadmaps, and portfolio roadmaps at www.svpg.com/examples.

Chapter 8:

PATTON'S ADVICE FOR PRODUCT MANAGERS

Managing By Objective

"Never tell people how to do things. Tell them what to do, and they will surprise you with their ingenuity."

– General George S. Patton, Jr.

General Patton was quite a character. From what I know of him, it sounds like he would have been quite a product manager. He's the source of countless quotes and advice, but I want to consider the above quote and how I think it applies to product managers in two very important ways.

First, on the receiving end, customers and users will very often try to tell you as product manager how your product should work, rather than what your product should do. We all have experienced this, as it's simple human nature for us to try to envision solutions to problems. But when a product manager focuses on what problem to solve, it's pretty amazing how many possibilities open up as to how to best solve the problem.

Customers and users really aren't in a position to come up with a good solution themselves. They just don't know what's possible, and it's also extremely hard to envision the solution in advance.

Also relevant is the other side of this point, where the product manager tells the user experience designers and engineers how to design and build the product, rather than telling them what the product needs to do. This is an especially common problem with user experience design. This problem is exacerbated by the fact that companies typically have too few design resources, and sometimes the product manager is in fact the only person available to do the interaction design.

Unfortunately, the skills for interaction design are very different from product management, and it's the rare product manager who's good at both. Another problem I see that complicates this is that, in many companies, the user experience design resources are part of a service organization where they're pulled in "as needed" to help with design after the spec is complete. The problem here is that this severely limits the contribution of a good designer. Designers are most valuable very early in the process, when the product manager is working to understand the target market and come up with a solution.

A product manager who (a) has a good appreciation for the role of user experience design, (b) is in a company that has the user experience design function staffed and available, (c) gives the user experience designer the latitude to come up with solutions that meet the needs, has a big advantage in coming up with winning products.

Strong user experience designers, especially interaction designers, are hard to find. There simply aren't enough good academic programs turning out these critically important people. But when you do find one, be sure to fully utilize her. Make the designer a key part of your product team, and include her in your customer visits, personas, product brainstorming, and in deciding your product strategy and roadmap. Let her explore alternative designs and listen closely to her input in terms of user behavior and preferences.

All of the above also applies with engineers. The engineering team doesn't appreciate the product manager spelling out the details of the implementation any more than the product manager wants the customer to dictate the specifics of the requirements. In my experience, this is somewhat less frequent because the line between product managers and engineers is fairly clear, but when I review specs I find that it still happens a great deal.

So the more latitude you can give your engineers and user experience designers in coming up with the solutions to the problems you are trying to solve, the more likely they will come up with something that customers will love.

Chapter 9:
DEPUTY PRODUCT MANAGERS

The Smartest Guy In The Room

As product people, we're essentially in the idea business. It's our job to come up with great ideas and then make them a reality. While this takes skill and practice, the main ingredient is something that I don't know how to teach. We depend on smart people for the smart ideas. Sometimes these ideas come from within ourselves, but if we depend only on ourselves for the smart ideas, we're severely limiting our potential universe of smart ideas.

Probably the single most important lesson I've learned in the product business is to start by seeking out the smartest people in the company. I've found that every organization has at least a few very smart people, and these people may hold the key to unlocking your company's potential—if you can find them. They're not always where you'd guess, and sometimes they're being hidden from you. I never cease to be amazed at how petty office politics, ego, xenophobia and insecurity can get in the way of something so potentially beneficial for a company.

When you do find these people, you can use them any number of ways. I like to consider these people "deputy product managers" and sometimes I even give them public recognition as such. Often I'll recruit these people to come join the product team.

To illustrate the many different corners of your company that may be hiding these people, here are some favorite examples from my own career. Every one of these examples is based on a real person, but I have changed their names.

Sam: It took me longer to find Sam than it should have because his manager was actively bad-mouthing him. However, it quickly became clear that it was the manager who was clueless, because what was really going on was that the manager was insecure and intimidated by Sam's mind. So not only had Sam not been recognized and utilized, he had actually been demoted! Today, that manager is history and Sam is one of the best product leaders I know.

Chris: I met Chris when I was out assisting a customer visit with HP, and our salespeople were making little sense when briefing us on the local considerations. Finally, an SE (systems engineer–they provide technical assistance to the sales staff) stepped in and did an outstanding job articulating what the situation was. I could see the respect that the customer had for the SE, and afterwards I invited him to grab a beer. It was soon very clear to me that I was sitting with an extremely talented guy. I asked him why he was hiding in the Midwest as an SE, and he explained he had family in the area, he had never thought of living elsewhere, and that he had taken the best job he could find. I immediately began to use Chris as a sounding board and source of product ideas and, while it took a while, I finally got him to relocate. Today he's a general manager at a Fortune 500 company. While engineers often have great insight into the available technologies, people from the field often have great insight into customer needs, which for Chris, combined to give him extraordinary insight into user problems plus the possible solutions.

Alex: As is so often the case, I found Alex deep in the ranks of an engineering team. He was shy and introverted, and not especially ambitious. But the guy was incredibly smart. He not only knew technologies extremely well, but he had a natural product sense, understood the broader technology trends, and he was a constant champion of the user experience. He's a great engineer, and people assumed that that represented his full potential. However, Alex had an equally talented product mind, and he was one of those rare people who are great at just about everything. He never made the move to product, but he did become one of the thought leaders in the company and was consulted on virtually every major product decision. And the company and the products we built were much better for it.

Matt: I wish it was not the case, but there are many forms of discrimination in business, even in high tech. But one form of discrimination that I had thought would have been long gone by now is discrimination due to youth. Matt is probably the most brilliant person I've ever worked with. He graduated college while still in his teens, and he never slowed down. But when I met Matt, he was dramatically underutilized because his manager couldn't imagine giving someone so young that much responsibility. Big mistake. Matt jumped ship and went on to co-found a startup that has improved the lives of millions.

Mira: This talented individual had it twice as tough—she was female and Indian. In this loud, heavily male, technology-driven industry, women are easily overlooked. And culturally, Indians are often quiet and reluctant to challenge authority—that of their managers or their colleagues. But Mira was easily the smartest "guy" in the room, and it didn't take long to draw her out of her shell and for her to establish herself as the product leader she was meant to be. I've seen this with Chinese nationals as well. Don't let cultural norms or an accent through you off—these may be the product minds you're searching for.

I've learned that sometimes the greatest product minds are right there in front of you. You may be at a company that's enjoyed some success, and the product mind that got you there is now CEO or chairman of the board, and seemingly unreachable to today's product team. If the founder is good, he's probably trying not to step in and micro-manage things himself, but that doesn't mean that he's not willing to help. If you're lucky enough to have great product people as founders, you should initiate a channel with them and invite their feedback and suggestions on your product plans. They're often all too happy to do so, and you should absolutely find a way to utilize that resource if it is available to you.

The bottom line is that these minds can be hidden anywhere—engineering, sales, customer service, professional services, the exec team, or your board of directors. It's your job to find them. Now—how do you do that?

- Ask! Ask at all levels of the company who people think the really great minds are, and you may be surprised by their answers.
- MBWA. From the HP Way—Management By Wandering Around. Managers need to get out of their office or cubes and spend time with the people from across the company, not in meetings, but informally. It's easy and it works.
- Listen (*really* listen) to the dialog in meetings and conversations.
- Keep your door open—make sure everyone knows that they are welcome to drop in with product suggestions.
- Share. If you are willing to share with others the issues that you're struggling with, you'll find that word will get around and people may stop by with suggestions.
- Hang Out. All too often the product people hang out with other product managers, and execs with other execs. But if you make an effort to spend time with people at all levels of your company, you'll get a much better idea of what's going on in general, and who the hidden gems are in particular.

Finally, the main reason why I think most product managers are not focused on the above is ego. They think that they are the ones that must always come up with the big ideas, and that if someone else did, what would their purpose be? While sometimes I come up with an idea I like, more often than not I get my inspiration or the core idea itself from others. You still need to be able to recognize that great idea, and make that idea a reality. Just remember that the only thing that really matters for your company is shipping great products. Anything that helps you do that is all good.

Chapter 10:

MANAGING UP

Top 10 List

One of the most common questions I get from product managers, most often at large companies, is how to manage their managers. They are frustrated with their managers— it's not that they don't like them, but they feel like the sands keep shifting. Their managers give them different and conflicting direction each week, and it's always two steps forward and one step back. Especially in big companies, there are so many influencers and stakeholders that getting a company to move in a single direction long enough to get a product out can be a true challenge.

There are many reasons for the constant change in direction. It's not just you and your manager who need to be on the same page, your manager's manager—and others on up the chain—all bring their own initiatives to the table. And there are outside influences as well, such as competitive pressures, changing technologies, mergers and acquisitions, business development deals, budget and staffing constraints, and more. Each of these can—and usually do—have a direct or indirect impact on your product plans. That's part of the cost of working at a large firm. The benefit, however, is that if you can find a way to leverage the resources of your large company, you can have a dramatic impact on the marketplace on a scale that's hard to match at a small firm.

Even in small companies and startups, these challenges exist. But I think that in large companies it is especially difficult. I have worked in product organizations large and small, at every level, and I've collected a list of techniques that have helped me with this problem. But I will say up front that the challenges are substantial and they won't go away; the best you can do is to mitigate the issues, and here are some ways to do that.

So here's my list of ten techniques for managing up:

1. Measure and plan for churn.

Churn is the term I use to represent the cost of the various drills, rework, and changes in plans that cause the frustration you feel in the first place. While you shouldn't expect churn to go down to zero, you can constantly strive to reduce it. This starts by increasing awareness of churn, and that begins with measuring it. There are lots of ways to do this, but in one form or another, try to track how much of your week/month/quarter is spent on forward progress. Now that you're more aware of the level of churn, it helps a great deal to plan for some amount of churn. When you're scheduling your projects, know that there will be a percentage of your time devoted to responding to these changes and adjusting accordingly, and that some amount of your efforts will end up sitting on the shelf. It will help manage your stress level, make your schedules more accurate, and help you identify issues you can try to improve.

2. Communication style and frequency.

Just as product managers are not all the same, managers are not all the same either. Some managers prefer to be kept apprised of every little detail on a continual basis. Others don't want you to bother them unless there's an escalation or serious issue that needs your manager's help. Some prefer updates in writing with detailed supporting material, and others prefer a quick chat in the hall. You need to determine the style that your manager prefers and do your best to meet that need, even if it's not your own preferred style.

3. Pre-meeting work.

Most product companies have lots of meetings—too many in my view. However, the more influencers and stakeholders there are in your organization, the more you'll be asked to have checkpoint and review meetings to keep everyone on track and informed. There are many techniques for running good meetings, but the main point here is to actually conduct the real meetings before your official meeting. This means going individually to the key influencers and stakeholders prior to the actual meeting and giving them a preview of your points, listening to their issues, and ensuring that they are already on board by the time the group meeting happens. If you do this well, the group meeting should be quick with no surprises. The formal meeting still has an important purpose however, which is for everyone at the table to see that everyone else is on board.

4. Recommendations, not issues.

Most managers prefer to see your recommendations on how to solve problems you encounter rather than just a statement of the problem. Ideally, depending on the size of the problem, this means an analysis of several alternatives along with your recommendation and rationale.

5. Use your manager.

Managers can often be a very useful tool that most employees underutilize. As an example, suppose there's a problem you're working to solve, and you have an analysis and recommendation, but some of the key influencers are not anxious to make the time available you need to pre-brief them as described in the pre-meeting work above. Your manager can often get the access you can't. So provide your manager with the tools and the request that she hold this private session for you. Your manager will want to be prepared, but is often happy to help in this way.

6. Do your homework.

One of the biggest mistakes product managers make is in not doing their homework. Managers are usually smart and can quickly identify holes in thinking and in plans—that's their job. The best way for you to prepare for this is by doing your homework. You need to understand the issues thoroughly and be prepared.

7. Short e-mails.

Another common mistake is that product managers like to write long, detailed e-mails to their managers, but then get frustrated when they're not read or responded to. You need to realize that your manager is probably getting hundreds of e-mails a day, and is looking for short, to-the-point communications. The more senior the person you're sending to, the shorter you'll want the e-mail to be. Offer additional material, but don't make the manager read more than a few lines.

8. Use data and facts, not opinions.

When dealing with managers—especially senior managers—it's essential to remember that your job is to provide the data and facts. Jim Barksdale, the former CEO of Netscape, had a great line when he was confronted with difficult decisions. He said, "If we're going to make this decision based on opinions, we're going to use my opinion." If you do your homework, and have collected and laid out the data, your recommendation should be clear based on the facts and not opinion.

9. Evangelize.

A big part of a product manager's job is to evangelize the product across the organization. But few product managers seem to take this as seriously as I think they should. If you evangelize effectively, everything will become easier—especially working with other groups in the company. If they know what you're doing and are excited about what your product will do for the company, they'll be much more likely to find ways to help.

10. Low-maintenance employees.

One of the secrets that nearly every manager thinks—but few will admit—is that what they're really looking for in an employee is someone who is low maintenance. High-maintenance employees consume a disproportionate amount of the manager's time and attention, and while it's your manager's job to ensure that his team is productive, there is only so much time in the day, and this type of hand-holding is not usually what your manager is anxious to spend his day doing. Don't try to use your manager as a mentor—find another mentor from outside of your direct management chain. And be thoughtful of how you use of your manager's time. I can promise you that your manager will appreciate it.

Many product managers get frustrated, especially in large companies. If this is your situation, give these techniques a try. You won't eliminate the issues, but hopefully you'll see a real improvement.

DILBERT: © Scott Adams/Dist. by United Feature Syndicate, Inc.

Activities and Best Practices

The processes and techniques used by today's top software and Internet companies are in many cases very different than those used by most companies.

This section describes the processes, activities, and best practices used to repeatedly discover and build inspiring and successful products.

Chapter 11:

ASSESSING PRODUCT OPPORTUNITIES

Defining The Problem To Be Solved

Opportunities for new products exist all around us, in every market—even mature markets. This is because what is possible is always changing. New technologies are constantly emerging, competitors come and go, and new people with new talents and new ideas join your company.

The product manager must be able to quickly evaluate opportunities to decide which are promising and which are not; what looks appealing, which should be pursued, which are better left for others, and which ideas are not yet ready for productization.

In many companies, the decree comes down from above, in something akin to, "We really need to do this product." In other companies, the marketing organization determines what products are needed. And in yet others, the ideas come from engineering.

Unfortunately, too often the process of deciding whether or not to build a product is left to intuition (or worse, a large customer will offer to fund a "special," and this becomes the basis for a product effort).

Typically someone on the business side or in marketing will create some form of a Market Requirements Document (MRD) that is intended to describe the problem to be solved and usually includes a business justification. The purpose of the MRD is to describe the opportunity, not the solution—at least, that's the theory. In practice, many companies don't really do MRDs, or if they do, they're essentially attempts at product specs that are misnamed as MRDs. Even if a true MRD is done, they suffer many of the same problems as PRDs—that is, they take too long to write, they aren't read, and they often don't answer the key questions they need to address.

The result is that many product managers ignore the MRD altogether. But there's a problem with not doing anything and just jumping right into the product: it is generally a good idea to look before you leap. The challenge is to do this in a quick, lightweight, yet effective manner.

I consider the Product Opportunity Assessment an extremely important responsibility of the product manager. The purpose of a good product opportunity assessment is to either (a) prevent the company from wasting time and money on poor opportunities by ultimately proving the idea should be shelved for now, or (b) for those opportunities that are good ones, focus the team and understand what will be required to succeed and how to define that success.

Fortunately, it's really not that hard to do a useful opportunity assessment. I ask product managers to answer ten fundamental questions:

1.   Exactly what problem will this solve? (value proposition)

2.   For whom do we solve that problem? (target market)

3.   How big is the opportunity? (market size)

4.   How will we measure success? (metrics/revenue strategy)

5.   What alternatives are out there now? (competitive landscape)

6.   Why are we best suited to pursue this? (our differentiator)

7. Why now? (market window)

8. How will we get this product to market? (go-to-market strategy)

9. What factors are critical to success? (solution requirements)

10. Given the above, what's the recommendation? (go or no-go)

Note that none of these questions speaks to the actual solution. This is both intentional and critically important. The opportunity assessment should just discuss the problem to be solved, not the particular solution you may have in mind. The majority of your time going forward will be focused on the solution, but this is the time to think clearly and concisely about the problem you are trying to solve.

All too often what happens is that a product manager combines the problem to be solved with the solution and, when they run into difficulties with the particular solution they are pursuing, they abandon the opportunity. It's a classic example of throwing the baby out with the bathwater.

The hardest question to answer is usually the first in the opportunity assessment, the value proposition, which surprises many people because it sounds like the easiest. But ask most product managers what problem their product is intended to solve, and you usually get a rambling list of features and capabilities, rather than the a crisp, clear and compelling statement of the exact problem that's being solved.

Another difficult problem can be assessing the size of the opportunity. You can get thoughts on this from industry analysts, trade associations, your finance staff, and from your own bottom-up calculations. Just remember to be conservative and realize that not every opportunity needs to be a billion-dollar market.

The go-to-market strategy is especially important as it describes how the product will be sold, which can have very significant impact on product requirements.

The success factors, or solution requirements, refer to any special needs or requirements that were identified during the investigation. Again, we're not describing the product here, but rather making clear any dependencies or constraints. For example, if this is a product that will be sold through system integrators, then these types of partners have requirements around extensibility of the products they deliver. Similarly, there may be branding or partnership requirements.

A product organization is all about pursuing good opportunities and providing great product solutions. Opportunities for new products are everywhere, and it is important that the product manager be able to effectively evaluate new opportunities and identify those that have the most potential for their company. It is just as important that bad product ideas get identified and rejected at this stage, before significant time and money is lost chasing them. Choosing the right set of products to pursue is among the most important decisions a company will make.

It is important that the results of the product opportunity assessment be presented and discussed with senior management, and that the company make a clear decision on whether or not to pursue a product to meet this opportunity. If you do decide to proceed, you will be much better informed about what you are getting yourself into, and what it will take to succeed.

So what do you do if the CEO tells you that, like it or not, this is what we're doing, so just get to work on the product? First, realize that there are sometimes strategic reasons for doing a particular product, so you might need to pursue it even when it's unlikely to succeed in the marketplace. That said, doing a lightweight and quick product opportunity assessment is still valuable because you will become much better informed about what the product involves. It is possible that what you learn will change your CEO's opinion, but even if not at least you will have a clear understanding of your objective.

 Build New Or Fix Old?

I'm often asked what the right balance is between new product development and improving existing products. I suppose it's natural for companies to want to have some sort of percentage guideline, but I try to get companies to think about these investments a little differently. To me, all projects, whether a new 1.0 product, or an enhancement to an existing product, are product investments and instead of worrying about whether you're investing enough in new product lines versus existing product lines, I would rather have the team worry about investing in the best opportunities.

Expanding your product offering so that you can offer additional products to existing customers or acquire new customers can be a great thing. Improving your existing products so that they generate more revenue from your existing customers plus make it easier to get new customers can also be a great thing.

The real key is that each of these projects is a product opportunity and, as such, it's the responsibility of the product team to assess the benefits and the costs. Then it's the responsibility of the management team (see the chapter *The Product Council*) to ensure the company is pursuing the best opportunities available. This might be completely or mostly new product opportunities, particularly for new companies, or it might be mostly product improvement opportunities for a more established business. It's not a bad thing to be opportunistic when it comes to choosing your product investments.

Many times, the best product opportunities are sitting right under the company's nose. In particular, often the biggest bang for the buck comes from improving existing products that are not performing at the level they should and could be. For example, you might find that for every 100 people who explicitly begin the subscription process for your product, only 9 make it through to successful completion. You know that if you can improve that number to 18, you've essentially doubled the revenue for that product. That's a great opportunity if you can find a good solution. And the ironic thing about this type of opportunity is that it is often the most straightforward to solve. With just a bit of prototyping and user testing, you can quickly identify the issues and come up with better solutions that are often not difficult to implement.

Here's another example: you may find that you're employing

hundreds of customer service staff to help your users as they struggle to configure and use your product. Improving the product's usability can significantly reduce the need for customer service staff—and that's just the cost savings. The even bigger win may be the improvement in customer satisfaction and your corresponding NPS score.

I often come into a company and look like a hero when I point out these "opportunities" and the big returns they can generate. But I think what's really going on is that there is a tendency in software companies to assume that the product is already about as good as it can be, and continued investment won't make much of a difference. Companies tend to believe that their products are inherently complex, or that a 9% conversion rate isn't bad, or that they just need to spend more on customer acquisition marketing or advertising, or that investing in customer service is just a necessary cost of doing business.

However, what's actually going on is that the product is weak, and the company is just trying to make the best of what they have.

On one level, this is just another symptom of companies under-investing in design and user experience. But more generally, the truth is that many products are poorly done and, rather than improve a product to the point where it can generate real revenue and success, many organizations view it as easier to create a new product instead. But unless they change the way they produce that new product, they're likely going to end up with yet another under-performing product in need of improvement.

Where's the Money?

Do you understand the economics of your product? Do you know your exact revenue model? Do you know the total costs of your product? Do you know how much you pay for each new customer? Do you know their lifetime value to the company? Do you know the return your product has generated for the company?

In my experience, most product managers—especially product managers with a technical background—have only a very shallow understanding of how their product (or their company) makes money. This is especially the case for those of us that came to product management from engineering.

I learned a long time ago that I could benefit a great deal from making a friend in the finance department. In every company I've ever worked at, I have asked the CFO for someone that could help me answer these questions. It always amazed me how willing these people were to help, and just how much information they had available for those who asked.

I've found that my friends in finance can help with three big things.

Understanding Your Product

Sit down with your friend and ask for help determining and evaluating the financial aspects of your product, starting with the questions I posed above. If you have partnerships, read the contracts. If you license technology, look at the agreements. Ask your friend to help you assess your product. Is it carrying its own weight? Is it a good investment for the company? What trends does your friend see? Is the product heading in the right direction?

Understanding Your Customers

While we typically have good tools for understanding how users behave on a Web site (via Web analytics), the finance department often has a wealth of additional information on the actual customers, accumulated from transaction histories, payment information, customer data, and management reporting. You both need to be sensitive about what information you can view and how you use it, but in terms of understanding your customers it can be extremely useful.

More than once I've uncovered information about my products from the financial staff that truly surprised me, and exposed fantastic opportunities. One time in particular I remember asking my friend in finance why nobody knew about one such opportunity, and he replied "Because nobody asked." Realize the life of a finance person is largely thankless, and driven by extreme deadlines ("Our quarter closes on Thursday and we're announcing earnings on Monday!"). I also have a theory that people in finance are often fairly quiet, and not the type to come to your desk advocating product opportunities. Usually, you've got to go to them.

Preparing The Business Case

You've got a great idea, but you're not sure about the business case—now what? Your friend in finance can help. You'll need to provide most of the inputs, but your friend will know how to put together the case. If it's a good case, you'll also find that having someone in finance who has studied the economics of the potential product can be a big help for you when discussing with senior management.

So go make a friend in finance. You need the information they have and their help in interpreting the information and putting it to good use. I think you'll find that these people want to help their company, and appreciate the opportunity to do so.

 Examples

You can see example opportunity assessments at www.svpg.com/ examples.

Chapter 12:
PRODUCT DISCOVERY

Defining The Right Product

Software projects can be thought of as having two distinct stages: figuring out what to build (build the *right product*), and building it (building the *product right*). The first stage is dominated by product discovery, and the second stage is all about execution.

When in product discovery, you welcome and explore new ideas, talk with scores of users and customers, learn how you can apply new technologies, flesh out your product concepts and test them out, and spend a lot of time thinking about the overall product direction, both immediate and longer term. It is all about discovering that mix of form and function that results in a winning product.

However, once you've spec'd out this product, and your engineering team begins the process of building it, a very profound and important shift needs to take place for the product team. Now the game is all about execution—getting the product built, tested, and delivered to market. In this stage, you spend your time keeping everyone focused, chasing down the countless issues that inevitably arise, and getting these issues resolved immediately. Acquisitions, competitors, organizational and management changes—these are all distractions, and your job is to keep the team on track so this product can get out there when it needs to be.

In countless product teams, this shift in mindset doesn't actually happen—or at least it doesn't happen until much later, often as late as entering QA. Instead, product managers continue to explore new ideas, and company execs continue to view the product spec as malleable. What results is euphemistically referred to as "churn," where the product spec continues to change in significant ways, impacting engineering and the rest of the product team. As a result, the release dates get pushed out, or features get cut, or the quality gets compromised. Or all the above.

If you're lucky enough to have a great project manager, then you probably have help keeping everything on track during execution. But even if you do, as a product manager you'll need to be cognizant of this necessary change in mindset; otherwise, it is all too easy for the product manager to be the source of the product's inability to get to market.

However, I think it's important to recognize that we all have our own unique preferences and skills. If you're naturally a discovery kind of person—preferring the freedom and creativity of the invention process—then you'll have to work extra hard to contain those urges during execution. On the other hand, if you're more naturally the project manager type who loves getting things out the door, then you'll need to work on your strategic thinking and discovery skills— remembering that what matters most is creating a product that your customers love.

One technique I have found very useful is to always keep two versions of a product going in parallel. In other words, as soon as you start the engineering for release 1.0 and switch into execution mode for that project, then you start up the discovery for release 2.0 in parallel. Always keep that innovation engine working—once a given release goes to engineering, redirect your creative urges to the next release.

One note of warning: You do need to be careful that this approach doesn't detract from the execution work for the current project.

Overall, I've found that having this outlet is a good thing. The next time a company exec drops by with a big, new requirement, rather than impacting the product you have in the oven, you already have the next release in the discovery stage and you can start the work of exploring the new requirement there.

I don't mean to make this all sound overly simple, but I do believe that with discipline it can be managed. It's essential that you develop both your discovery skills (to ensure you're coming up with winning products) as well as your execution skills (to ensure that these great ideas actually make it to your customers).

 Can You Schedule Discovery?

Have you experienced this situation before? Your company gets all excited about a product idea, and as product manager you are asked to define it. You are told that the engineers will be finished with their current project in four weeks, so that means you can take all the time you need—so long as you are ready in four weeks.

No problem, you say (after all, sometimes you're only given days, so four weeks sounds great). You'll start with an opportunity assessment to understand the problem to be solved, then you'll spend quality time interviewing real users, and identify a preliminary set of requirements. By the start of the second week, you should be able to work with an interaction designer on a prototype, in the third week, you'll do user testing with the prototype and, in the fourth week, you'll flesh out the details of the use cases and review the prototype and spec with engineering.

These are all great practices. But what happens isn't usually so great. During your initial user discussions, you find that users aren't as excited about the idea as your management is, and/or you struggle to come up with a prototype that users can figure out, and/or the users aren't excited about the ideas in the prototype when they try it.

But time is up, the engineers are ready, so you give them what you have.

The result? During the next three to six months, engineering proceeds to build that same unusable and unexciting product that you saw in your prototype, you ship it, and then your management is of course disappointed with the results.

The problem isn't the reliability of the software, so the engineering team isn't to blame—after all, they just built what you asked them to. So whose fault is it? Everyone knows it's your fault—you're the product manager.

It doesn't help to talk to users, create prototypes, and test with users, if you don't adjust your course based on what you learn.

This notion of requirements and design as a sequential, predictable and scheduled phase in a product development process is so ingrained in our industry that it's often one of the most difficult habits for product organizations to break. But we all need to get past this. Product organizations need to come to terms with the fact that the product invention process is fundamentally a creative process. It is more art than science.

This is why I prefer to think of this phase as "product discovery" more than "requirements and design." I think this nomenclature emphasizes two all-important points:

First, you need to discover whether there are real users out there who want this product. In other words, you need to identify your market and validate the opportunity with your customers.

Second, you need to discover a product solution to this problem that is valuable, usable, and feasible. In other words, you need to design your solution and validate it with your customers and your engineering team.

Sometimes the product discovery phase is straightforward. Other times it is extremely difficult. In my experience, it's not so hard to discover and validate the market opportunity, but it's often very challenging to discover the solution. Even with the help of great designers and great engineers, some problems are just truly hard (at least many of the ones worth pursuing and that haven't been solved already).

The pharmaceutical drug industry provides an extreme example. The market discovery process is usually not very difficult—there are no shortage of good medical problems worth solving (like saving your life, extending your life, or improving the quality of your life). The hard part of course is discovering a product solution. Drug companies go into this discovery phase fully aware that there's no guarantee they'll come up with anything or, if they do, how long it may take. As an industry, they have come to terms with this element of uncertainty (and this risk is priced into their products).

Yet with software, even though we all know it is very hard—and we know that the majority of software releases fail to meet their objectives—we still insist on scheduling the discovery phase like we're planning the construction of a house.

Management especially struggles with this notion of product discovery. I think there are two underlying reasons for this:

First, the discovery process isn't as predictable as we wish it was. Management fears you may spend months chasing a solution and end up with nothing to show for it. At least if they go ahead and build, they can say that they shipped something. It's the same reason why many managers are uncomfortable with *Agile* methods like *Scrum*. They want to know how many 30-day sprints it will take before they're done.

Second, the most highly constrained and expensive resource in just about every software product organization is the engineers, and the thought that an engineering team might be sitting around with nothing to do but play Foosball just drives management nuts.

Ironically, it is precisely this reasoning that leads directly to wasted engineering resources.

Realize that almost every company executes the discovery process I've described here, only instead of using one prototyper for a few weeks, they use the full engineering team for full release cycles to build the software that is then QA'd and deployed into production systems. They are using the engineering organization to build a very, very expensive prototype, and they use their live customers as unwitting test subjects. This is also why it typically takes companies three or more releases over one to two years to get something they can make money from.

This is also a big reason why so many startups fail. Most startups simply don't have the funding to go two years before they gain traction in the marketplace. So they hire engineers, take their best shot, and see what happens. Ready, fire, aim.

Startups especially must focus their energies on this much faster product discovery process. And once they discover the solution that works—one that is valuable, usable and feasible—then it's all about execution. Until that point, they don't have to hire too many engineers right away—the engineers they already have can and should actively participate in the product discovery process. And, to a degree, the engineers can prepare the infrastructure while this discovery is going on.

You can help your management understand the nature of the product discovery process. If you consistently emphasize your obligation to ensure that what engineering builds must be valuable and usable, as well as enlist their efforts to discover a successful solution, you'll start to move their focus to this—the most critical stage of the product development process.

Chapter 13:
PRODUCT PRINCIPLES

Deciding What's Important

Another tool that can be a big aid in determining the right trade-offs and priorities is a good set of product principles. The product principles are a public declaration of your beliefs and intentions. I like them because if they're done well, they can serve as a useful complement to a product strategy and significantly speed the product discovery process.

When I start working with a product team, once I understand the business strategy, often one of the first activities we do together is to define a set of product principles.

Coming up with product principles means deciding what is important to you—and what is incidental—and deciding what is strategic and fundamental, and what is simply tactical and temporary.

There are other benefits to developing product principles. The process serves as a way for me to understand the DNA of a company, and what the founders hope to achieve. Most importantly, it serves as a framework for evaluating the many alternatives in front of every product and company.

Product principles are not a list of features and, in fact, are not tied to any one product incarnation. In this sense, they are most aligned with a product strategy for an entire product line, or with a company mission statement for a startup. A good set of principles serves as the basis or foundation for inspiring product features.

An example of a product principle for a movie site may be that the team believes that the user community's opinions on movies are more valuable than those of professional reviewers. Later, if a studio wants to place reviews on your site, you can then decide if this is consistent with your principles or not.

Whether you choose to go public with your product principles depends on your purpose. Often the principles are simply a tool for the product team, much like a product strategy document. But, in other cases, the principles serve as a clear statement of what you believe, intended for your users, customers, partners, suppliers, investors, and employees.

Another benefit I have found is that more than any other document, a set of product principles can bring together the product team—especially product management, user experience design, engineering, and marketing—and get the team on the same page.

While there's value in identifying your guiding product principles, you also need to prioritize them. Countless products are trying to be easy to use and also safe and secure. But what matters is the priority. Is ease of use paramount? Or is safety and security the primary concern?

Finally, many teams make a couple of mistakes when they first try creating a set of product principles. The first is that they state principles that are so generic that they aren't really useful ("must be reliable"). The second is that they confuse their product principles with design principles. For example, a common design principle is to provide a well-lit path (so the user always knows where to go next). That's not a product principle.

So, if you don't yet have a clear statement of the beliefs and principles that guide your product team, consider getting the team together for a couple hours to discuss, identify, and prioritize what you think is important.

 ## Resolving Conflicts

Quite a few product managers tell me that they're constantly struggling with endless meetings without structure or decisions, second guessing of earlier decisions, vetoes, politics and what I call "drive-bys" (when a manager drops in every so often, shoots down your progress, and then is gone again without providing the feedback or guidance that could help you address her concerns).

While this type of situation can occur with virtually any decision a company must make, I think this is an especially common problem with product decisions. As I see it, there are several reasons for this. First, everyone has an opinion about the company's products— they're probably what attracted them to join the company in the first place. Second, everyone feels strongly about the product since—at some level—we all realize that companies need money to survive, money comes from customers, and customers come for the products. Third, many of your colleagues view themselves as much more like your target customer than they really are (or think they understand the target customer much more than they really do).

Combine this with the fact that—in most organizations—the product team doesn't actually report into the product manager and so has little organizational power to coerce; the product manager must persuade the team and not dictate to it. The result is what makes product management so difficult and at times extremely frustrating.

In some teams, the product decision process can become so contentious and deadlocked that the decision must be escalated to a senior manager in order to move forward. If this happens (and sometimes it is unavoidable), I consider this to be a very bad result. You want the debate and the arguments, but you want everyone on board at the end. In most cases, a much better product will result. A senior manager can always make the call for you but, besides the resentment this creates, the product is the biggest loser.

I suppose it's little surprise that so many struggle to find an effective process for making product decisions.

I will not pretend that there's a way to make the product discovery process painless—there isn't. Constructive debate and argument is an essential ingredient to coming up with a great product. While I know those arguments are necessary, it doesn't mean I always enjoy them.

That said, as product manager you can make a very significant impact on this process—minimizing churn and maximizing creativity and quality of the result by doing the following:

For virtually all product decisions, the key is to properly frame the decision to be made, and to first get everyone on the same page in terms of:

- What problem exactly are you trying to solve?
- Who exactly are you trying to solve this problem for—which persona?
- What are the goals you are trying to satisfy with this product?
- What is the relative priority of each goal?

In my experience, most of the time when there's strong disagreement within the product team, it's not really over the facts of the situation—it's instead because each person has a different interpretation or weighting of the goals and the priorities.

For example, you should be arguing about what's most important to your target user: ease of use, speed, functionality, cost, security, privacy—this is the right argument. Once you've agreed on what the goals are and who exactly you want to satisfy—and, just as important, the relative priority—then you all have a common basis for evaluating and assessing the options.

It is extremely important to take prioritization seriously—you should get the team to agree on the specific ordering, most to least important. Don't just wave your hands and group the goals into something like "critical" and "very important." Be sure your team can identify what is most critical, then second most critical, and so on.

When I am called in on controversial product decisions, all too often the group has skipped this step, and is deep in the weeds of each option—everyone passionately arguing his or her case but without a common basis for evaluation. Everyone assumes the objectives and the priority. Even if you have done a great job developing these objectives, you should remind the team prior to the decision process. Put it up on the white board so that the team can see the exact framework for evaluating the options and making the decision.

Moreover, I think it is very important for product managers to be completely transparent in their decision making process and reasoning. You don't want the team thinking that you're just following your intuition. Every member of the team should be able to see the goals and objectives you are using, their priority, and how you assess each option. The decision—and the reasoning behind how you got there—should be clear to all.

So the next time you find your product team battling it out and getting into an unproductive and demoralizing state, bring the team back from the edge, and revisit the goals and priorities. Make sure you're all on the same page before returning to evaluating the different options.

 Examples

You can see example product principles at: www.svpg.com/examples.

Chapter 14:
THE PRODUCT COUNCIL

Timely And Definitive Product Decisions

Even in small companies, getting decisions made is often time consuming and frustrating. Every product company needs a mechanism to get the key stakeholders and decision makers together to make timely and informed product decisions.

My favorite way to ensure this is to establish a product council.

In general, I really am not a fan of committees or even most meetings. But I have found product councils to be very valuable, and their use can speed up the overall product development process considerably. This is because key product decision makers are all available with the express purpose of making those decisions the product organization needs to get products to market.

The challenge is to do this in a way that provides the visibility and oversight that management needs and is responsible for, without the micromanaging (and disempowerment) that comes with company executives trying to design products.

Many companies have some variations of this, but I credit the origin of the concept as described here to Maynard Webb, the former COO of eBay. I've worked with several companies since then to refine and streamline the specific responsibilities.

Purpose

The purpose of the product council is to set the strategic product direction, allocate product resources and investments, and provide a level of oversight of the company's product efforts. This group is not trying to set the company's business strategy, but rather—given the business strategy—come up with a product strategy that will meet the needs of the business. The decisions this group makes will directly impact the success of the business.

Membership

The Product Council is typically comprised of the cross-functional set of managers responsible for product development. Every company has its own considerations, but an example might be:

- CEO, COO or Division GM
- VP/Director of Product Management
- VP/Director of User Experience Design
- VP/Director of Marketing
- VP/Director of Engineering
- VP/Director of Site Operations
- VP/Director of Customer Service

As with any such group, the effectiveness of the meetings will largely be a function of the meeting skills of the leader. The leader needs to be good at staying on task, framing issues, and driving to decisions. Usually, the leader of the product council is either the head of product or—for smaller companies—the head of the company.

Make sure you have representation from the key areas, but try to keep the group at 10 or less. If more people want to be members (they will) make sure they each know who is there to represent their views. For example, the VP Sales might use the VP Marketing, and the head of QA might use the VP Engineering.

Specific Responsibilities

This is not a group that designs or builds products. This group should oversee the flow of products through the product development process, and make the key decisions required.

For each product effort, there are four major milestones for product council review and decision making:

Milestone 1: Review proposed product strategies and product roadmaps, and initiate opportunity assessments for specific product releases. That is, select the product opportunities to be investigated.

Milestone 2: Review opportunity assessments and recommendations, and issue go/no-go decisions to begin discovering a solution.

Milestone 3: Review product prototypes, user testing results and detailed cost estimates, and issue go/no-go decision to begin engineering.

Milestone 4: Review final product, QA status, launch plans, and community impact assessments, and issue go/no-go decision to launch.

Additional Notes

- For small organizations, one product council typically covers all products. For large companies, the product council typically aligns with the business unit.
- There is no need to review minor updates or fixes in this process—there should be an expedited process for the minor changes needed to run the business (which are typically more content related).
- These are not product design sessions—if there are issues with the product then the team should work on them and return to the product council when they have been addressed.

- While you will often have a very preliminary sense of estimated cost at Milestone 2, no one should take that estimate very seriously as the solution has not yet been outlined—anything beyond "small, medium or large" effort is not fair to engineering. However, the estimate of time and cost at Milestone 3 should be detailed, and something the full product team is prepared to commit to.

- You will need to decide if this group will also address issues of policy (such as product end-of-life policy, privacy policies, etc.) Often, this group does discuss such issues, but these topics can become long unstructured discussions if not managed. Make sure policy discussions don't delay product oversight responsibilities.

- The frequency of meetings depends on the number of product efforts going on. You may only need to meet for one hour a month, or you may need to meet two hours a week.

- It can be useful for the product council to review the business performance of the products that have launched. The product council may request a presentation on the business results of the product launch, typically 3-6 months post-launch. This sort of accountability will help the council better understand which investments and decisions they made were good ones, and why.

- Ideally, the product manager should present his product to the product council. His manager should help him prepare for this presentation, to ensure that he has done his homework and the recommendations are sound. The smart product manager will have individually briefed the members of the product council prior to his presentation to learn of any issues and resolve them, so he's not caught by surprise.

If you find your product organization taking too long to make decisions, consider instituting a product council. Hopefully you'll find that this one meeting eliminates countless others and makes the decision process informed, transparent and timely.

 ## When Do We Estimate Project Costs?

Even though we've been estimating project costs since the very beginning of software development, it's remarkable to me how much confusion remains. I believe the root cause of this confusion is that management needs cost information very early in the process, yet engineering doesn't have the information it needs for a reasonably accurate estimate until much later in the process (because there's virtually no good information yet on the solution required). The result is either premature estimates that prove wildly inaccurate, or surprises because people had different assumptions all along and—when the accurate estimate eventually does come in—management experiences a severe case of sticker shock.

Here's the process that I advocate—while it is intertwined with the product development process I support, it can also be applied in most situations.

Recall that I strongly encourage all product efforts to start with a 10-question opportunity assessment (see the chapter *Opportunity Assessments*). This assessment is what the management team uses to decide whether there is a problem worth trying to solve. There's no solution yet, just a problem and an opportunity. But, for most teams, there's a clear need at this stage for a very preliminary estimate of project scope. Of course, since there's no solution spelled out at this stage, it's going to be very much a SWAG (a "scientific wild-assed guess") which is why I recommend that the estimates at this stage be limited to "Small," "Medium," or "Large." It's usually fairly clear at this granularity what the cost will be, although there will still be occasional surprises.

If the opportunity looks good relative to the estimated cost, management will likely allow the project to proceed to defining the solution. It is at this stage that the product solution is spelled out in detail, ideally with a high-fidelity prototype that you validate against real target users with prototype testing.

Throughout the process of coming up with the solution, the product manager and interaction designer should include a member of engineering to evaluate the various options and estimate costs for the different alternatives. This information is then considered by the product manager and designer and the product is adjusted as needed. But at the end of the spec process, there should be a very detailed and high-confidence estimate based on a detailed description of the product proposed to be built.

At this stage, the management team has a detailed product spec, and a corresponding high-confidence cost estimate, and they should be able to make a final decision on whether to proceed to build this product or not. It may be that the solution turned out to be more complex and expensive than they thought, or they might not like the actual solution, but if they do proceed the entire product team knows the cost and the product they'll get for that investment.

To summarize, I'm suggesting a preliminary estimate at opportunity assessment time, followed by a detailed estimate that accompanies the final product spec.

Chapter 15:

CHARTER USER PROGRAMS

Your Product Development Partners

Most marketing people will tell you that nothing is more important or compelling when launching a product than to have a solid set of reference customers (or reference applications for a platform product). Yet it continually amazes me how many products launch with none.

If at launch there are a half-dozen marquee names publicly stating their use and satisfaction with a product, then the job of the sales and marketing folks is dramatically easier, as the greatest risk the potential customer faces is dramatically reduced. On the other hand, if good reference customers are missing, all the creative marketing and clever sales tactics in the world will only take you so far.

If there are no references, this is a huge red flag, and it usually means the product is either bad, or not yet ready for prime time. And you don't want to be the first to try to use it.

If there's only one or a few reference sites, I worry that what's been built is essentially a special, or custom solution, and that it won't be generally useful.

Note that this applies whether we're talking a platform technology, a business application, or even a consumer Internet service. Potential customers need to know that this product really works for people like them.

Now let's move for a moment from our focus on the launch to the very beginning of the project.

As product manager, you know your job is to gain a deep understanding of your target customer, the problems to be solved, and whether you can come up with a product that meets these needs. You know you need to work closely and directly with customers to develop a product that will meet the needs of hundreds of customers (and thousands—or even millions—of users), but you also know there aren't enough hours in the day to work directly with this many customers.

My favorite technique for addressing both of these problems— getting deep insight into my target customers, and having great reference customers at launch—is to use a charter user program (also known as a Customer Advisory Board, Customer Council, or Voice of the Customer). This is not a new technique (I did my first at HP about 20 years ago), and many companies do this. But I'm surprised how many do not.

The program is fairly straightforward. Your goal is to end with at least six happy, live, referenceable customers from your target market. That means you'll probably need to start with 8-10. So your job is to recruit these customers right at the start of your project. You're looking for customers in your target market who would make great references. They may be from your existing customer base, or prospects, or often a blend of both. The key is that they believe this is a real problem to solve and they need it solved as quickly as possible.

Here's the deal:

The benefits to the customers/users that join:

- They get early and significant product input—they recognize the problem that this product is trying to solve, they feel the pain, and are anxious to ensure they find a good solution

- They get early access to the product—again, they feel the pain, so the sooner they can get relief the better
- Typically, there is a significantly reduced cost, if any

The benefits to you:

- You have a set of users and customers available for ongoing questions and dialog
- You have access to the customer's offices and the users at that company (or the company's developers if it's a platform product)
- The customers/users agree to come to your offices periodically for group sessions
- The customer agrees to deploy test versions promptly and provide timely feedback (you'll typically be there with them)
- If they are happy with the delivered product, the customer agrees to serve as a public reference customer

A few critical points:

- It's important that the customer *not* pay in advance to participate in this program. That would make this a very different type of relationship. You want a partner in developing the product—you do not want to build a custom solution just for them, and you're not a project shop. You can take their money after you deliver them a product they love.
- If you're like most companies, you will be overwhelmed with customers that want to participate. It really is a great deal, and customers know this. If you have a sales organization, they'll try to use this as a bargaining chip, and the result is that you'll be leaned on to include many more customers

than you can handle. This will take finesse at times, but it's important that the members of the charter user program be the right set. (Sometimes companies create an early release program that is available for those customers that want the software early, but aren't right for the charter user program. This is fine. Just make sure you don't accept more than about 10 customers into the charter user program as you won't be able to manage them and work as closely as you need to with that many.)

- If you find that you are having real trouble recruiting charter users and customers, then it's very likely you are chasing a problem that isn't that important, and you will probably have a very hard time selling this product. This is one of the very first reality checks to make sure you are spending your time on something worthwhile. If customers aren't interested in this problem, you may want to rethink your plans.

- You need to make sure your charter users and customers are truly from your target market. It's easy to end up with early adopters, who are much more tolerant and can easily lead to a product of interest only to early adopters (See the chapter *Emotional Adoption Curve*).

- You will need to explain to each member of the program that you are trying to come up with a general product— something you can successfully sell to a large number of customers. You're not trying to build a custom solution that works only for that particular company, and they wouldn't really want that in any case (because if you can't build a real business with that product, you'll go under and they'll be left with unsupported, dead-end software). You are, however, deeply committed to coming up with a product that works very well for them.

- You need to think of these charter users and customers as development partners. You're in this together. You need to treat them as colleagues. You are helping each other. You'll find that the relationships you create can last for decades.

- You will be interacting with these people throughout the project lifecycle—you'll be showing them prototypes and testing with their users, you'll be asking hundreds of detailed questions, and you'll be testing release candidates in their environment.

- Make sure you release the software to these people before the general release, and make sure they are live and happy before the public release. When you launch, they'll be ready to stand up for you.

- You'll likely be working very closely with product marketing on preparing the charter customer to be a public reference, and they'll often help with finding these partners as well.

- If your product is a platform product (others will write and deliver applications on top of your product), then this program is especially critical. The main difference is that you want to focus on ending the program with six reference applications rather than six customers. And you'll need to work closely with your application partners to ensure that the applications they build on your platform are also successful with their users (and a great way to do that is to encourage them to have charter users).

Note that while many of my examples are for customers in an enterprise software or a platform product sense, these techniques also work with end-users for consumer Internet services and consumer devices. For consumer services, you will want to expand the set to 10-15 or so, but the key is to really get to know these people and the environment in which they will be using your product—home or office. It is all too easy when designing a site for consumers to not have enough exposure to true target users until very late in the process (beta or even launch). This is very dangerous, and a program like this helps keep the product manager focused on providing real value to real users. In terms of marketing, when consumers decide to buy or use a product, they may not look at reference customers the same way a business purchaser would, but consumers are influenced by the press and user review sites, and when the press writes a story about your product, the first thing they'll look for is real users.

This really is an easy and powerful technique to ensure that you're building a product that customers want, and that you can prove to prospective customers that they're likely to be successful and happy if they go with you.

Don't Talk To Customers?

Every so often I meet a product manager who tells me she is not allowed to talk to users or customers. Sometimes it's because the sales reps want to control all such access, or maybe it's because marketing is supposed to be the interface with the customer, or perhaps the product is sold through a channel. Occasionally, there is a corporate policy restricting direct customer access because of worries about inappropriate statements or commitments. Whatever the reason, if you work at a company where you're told you can't talk to your users, my advice is to first try hard to change this policy. If that doesn't work, dust off your resume and find a place where you can practice your craft and have a shot at creating successful products.

I really don't know how you can build products users will love without a deep understanding of those users, and you won't get that without lots of direct communication—including face-to-face interactions.

Often, especially in larger companies, there are many different filters set up to try to "help" you as product manager understand the market. You'll find marketing groups that commission surveys and focus groups that produce reports on what users (think) they want, and sales organizations that will have someone like a sales engineer (technical assistant to sales reps) designated to aggregate customer input and pass it along to the product manager. Or you'll find customer service managers who are responsible for monthly reports on the top issues.

All that input is fine, but it is in no way a substitute for the product manager getting the direct interaction with users he needs to do his job.

To be very clear, I believe that the product manager should attend every user interview, every site visit, every usability test, and every charter user program meeting that pertains directly to his product.

It is from getting to know enough of these people—and digging with each of them into their underlying needs—that we get the insights necessary to discover great products. The insights won't come from the surface level dialog of "I need to customize this page, and get a report with the time spent divided by the number of resources," or, "72% of our users said they want higher-resolution videos."

By all means, leverage your organization. Many marketing organizations have user research capabilities that can be a huge help in facilitating and analyzing user interactions. Just make sure you're there working with the researcher. It's also fine to bring along a marketing person so she can start thinking about messaging and positioning. And I'm a fan of bringing along the lead engineer so he can start thinking about how these underlying issues might be solved.

But don't abdicate your responsibility to understand the user.

One final point: As you meet users, you'll start to naturally find that some are much more useful to you than others in terms of fitting your target profile, or the level of insight they can provide. For these people, establish an ongoing relationship. Get their phone number and e-mail address and keep them handy in your office. They might be great candidates for the charter user program, or at the least you can use them for additional user testing.

Chapter 16:
MARKET RESEARCH

Understanding The Capabilities And Limitations

If your company is like most, there's some amount of natural tension between marketing and product. One often controversial topic is the appropriate role in product discovery of market research tools and techniques such as focus groups, customer surveys, site analytics, site visits, usability testing/field testing and competitive analysis.

Unfortunately, I think this is an area of significant confusion, fueled in part by the various camps—those from a marketing background that may see the benefits of these tools, and those from product that see the limitations. The result is that some product teams miss out because they don't take advantage of the information these tools and techniques can offer. Yet other teams go astray because they depend on these techniques to answer questions the tools are incapable of answering.

This is a big topic, but I'd like to discuss the major market research tools and consider how they can help you—and where they can't.

The tools for market research have improved dramatically in the past decade. Many of the concerns of the past—which I'll discuss shortly—are addressed by new technologies for easily reaching out to large numbers of users and customers. These technologies can also help you analyze your user's activity and behavior—who they are and what they do with your product. That said, there are still some very fundamental, inherent limitations to market research tools, so it's important to understand that too.

Capabilities

Let's begin with a summary of the main tools and techniques:

Customer surveys. The Web has made this approach easy and powerful. Combined with techniques such as conjoint analysis (to help users rank order their preferences), customer surveys are so easy and so inexpensive, that they're a must-do for any product. However, there are two important things to note. First, there is an art to coming up with the survey questions themselves—it's not as easy as it sounds. Think hard about the questions and context, otherwise you'll find that people in your company will discount the results. They'll argue "garbage in, garbage out," which may very well be true if the questions are unclear or biased in their phrasing. Second, set expectations in your company that this data is but one input to the answer—it isn't the answer itself. You may very well have every user come back and say "I want X" and it still may make more sense for your company to instead give them "Y."

Site analytics. If your product is a Web site, there are terrific tools out there for understanding how your users are using it. You'll have to do a little work to make sure your site is instrumented appropriately, but it's well worth it. Get the site analytics in place early and continually watch and learn—and adjust. If your product is not a Web site, you can usually instrument your product so that it records valuable information about how the product is used and sends the data to you. You may have to be clear to your customers that you're sending aggregated data and nothing personally identifiable, but it's worth getting it.

Data mining. You'll collect data from many sources, such as the site analytics I've mentioned above, billing and user account information, and your own product's data. Today there are better tools than ever for analyzing and harvesting that data. Want to know the gender breakdown of people that use some combination of your services? Or the activity level tiers and distribution of a specific persona? You can usually answer these and thousands of other questions easily and quickly with the new breed of data analysis tools.

Site visits. There is no real substitute for visiting with your users in their native habitat—home, office, mall—wherever they will use your product. It can be expensive and time-consuming yet, whenever I do a site visit, I realize something I wouldn't have known any other way. Site visits are extremely valuable, but for cost and time considerations you'll want to pick them carefully.

Personas. I like personas, especially for product definition and design. Market researchers use personas too, although not for the same purposes. It's essential to realize that there is no single "user" and your job is to deeply understand the major types of users out there—those who are your current customers, and those you want to have in the future. See the chapter *Personas for Product Management.*

Usability testing. I am a huge fan of usability testing, and advocate its use early and often (see the chapter *Prototype Testing*). You can also use this tool with existing products to better understand what users really think. Essentially, it's a way to see through their eyes while they use your product—you can gauge enthusiasm or frustration, and watch actions (and not just words). There are tools for doing this remotely, and for recording and analyzing what exactly people do, but this is all just icing on the cake.

Competitive analysis. Too frequently product teams write off competitors as clueless, but in my experience every product has at least some things that the product does well, and it's your job to find these things. Learn from their successes and their mistakes.

With these tools and techniques you can get some very real help answering the following important product questions:

- Do you understand who your users really are?
- How are users using your product?
- Can users figure out how to use your product? Where do they stumble?
- Why do users use your product?
- What do users like about your product?
- What do users want added to or changed in your product?

Limitations

Notice that while these questions are critically important, they do not directly address the fundamental question for most product people: What product to build?

This information certainly is an input to the product creation process, but you're in trouble if you try to steer your product with market research.

The product discovery process is about answering these questions:

- What technologies can I apply to solve this problem in a better way?
- What should the user experience be?

As useful as market research tools and techniques are, I know of no winning product that was created by market research. Not Google, not eBay, not the iPod or iPhone, not FaceBook or MySpace. None.

Winning products come from the deep understanding of the user's needs combined with an equally deep understanding of what's just now possible.

I wish we could simply ask customers what they want, but if you do that you'll end up with incremental and evolutionary improvements to what they already have (at best) or—more likely—a random collection of band-aid features, and not the new and dramatically better solution that you're looking for.

If you've already launched your product, and if you have a set of active customers, you can learn a great deal from talking to them about what parts they like—and what parts they don't—and get their views on incremental features. The key is to understand the limitations of each, and that this data is about refining an existing product rather than conceiving a new one.

So by all means use market research tools to help refine your product and make it as good as it can possibly be. Just don't expect the techniques to produce the idea for the next Facebook, Flickr, or YouTube.

What About Focus Groups?

One tool I did not mention above is focus groups. That's because I have very mixed feelings about focus groups. I like anything that puts the product manager in front of his target users and customers, and it is possible for focus groups to do that. If handled well, there are benefits to be had.

That said, while you can learn about your target customers, I can promise you that you won't discover great products from focus groups. How come?

There are two very fundamental reasons why not:

1. Customers don't know what's possible. Most have no idea about the enabling technologies involved.

2. Customers don't know what they want. It's very hard to envision the solution you want without actually seeing it.

There are other drawbacks to focus groups:

First, there is a dynamic that happens when users get together. They influence each other so much that you lose the pure input of each, and instead get a skewed representation influenced by the most articulate or vocal attendees.

Second, related to the point about customers not knowing what they want, it's very hard to get useful data about a product idea unless customers can actually see and interact with the product. Most often, focus groups are conducted prior to the stage where that is possible.

Third, as with surveys, there is an art to conducting focus groups, and finding someone who actually knows how to conduct them effectively, and when they should and should not be used. Add a requirement to understand your product domain enough to elicit the depth of conversation you need, and it can be tough finding the right person for the job.

As a result, too often focus groups are used for political purposes rather than to get that deep understanding of users that you're looking for.

If you feel you must conduct focus groups, make sure the product manager attends every one in person. It is okay to delegate the logistics and the facilitation to an outside firm, but do not delegate the interpretation and analysis of the data.

Chapter 17:
PERSONAS FOR PRODUCT MANAGEMENT

Understanding The Target User

Product management is all about choices—making decisions about what opportunities are worth chasing, which problems are worth solving, what features will provide the most value, what the best time-to-market trade-offs are, and which customers are most important. While you'll never make all the right choices, you have to make most of them right for your product to succeed.

One of my favorite tools for helping to make the hard decisions is a *persona* (aka user profile)—a technique for capturing the important learnings from interviewing users and customers, and identifying and understanding the different types of people who will be using your product. The persona is an archetype description of an imaginary but very plausible user that personifies these traits—especially their behaviors, attitudes, and goals.

The tool was first described in 1998 in one of my all-time favorite books, *The Inmates Are Running the Asylum*, by Alan Cooper. If you haven't read this book you should—it's a classic for product managers, designers, and engineers.

There's a good chance that your designers already use personas in the design process. The design community seems to have adopted this technique as most of the design teams I meet use this tool. Each has their own spin on what makes a great persona, and some are much more formal about them than others, but in my view they're all good.

And there's even a chance your marketing people use personas as they create their messaging and advertising programs. These uses of personas are similar—and they're both useful—but they're not quite the same thing as they are used for somewhat different purposes. The marketing folks are trying to determine the best ways to reach the target customers and appeal to the underlying emotions. The designers care most about the user's goals and online behaviors.

As product manager, this is all extremely useful to you.

Unfortunately, while this is a truly powerful tool, it is often not employed until later in the product definition/discovery process than it should be. Often it is the designers who drive this, and they are all too often brought into the process later than they should be.

To get the true potential of personas, the product manager needs to be deeply involved in their creation and prioritization, and especially the user interviews and research that goes into identifying them. The creation of personas should be a collaboration between the product manager and interaction designer and—if you are lucky enough to have them—your user research team. But whatever you do, don't delegate this task. For the same reason that the product manager needs to be present at every usability test of his product, he or she needs to be at every user interview. The product manager needs that deep understanding of the target user that comes from talking with as many users and customers as possible.

I always encourage product managers to actively participate in the creation of personas—and make sure they are done as early in the process as possible.

The design community has written extensively about personas

so I won't try to duplicate all the details here, other than to point out some issues as they relate to product managers. For a detailed description, see the book *About Face 3* by Alan Cooper.

There are numerous benefits of using personas as a tool for product management:

- Personas help you prioritize what's important. If you have decided to make "Mary" the target for this release, then if this feature is critical for "Mary" then put it in, if it's for "Sam" then it's out. As you can see, just as important as deciding who a release is for, is deciding who it is not for. It is an extremely common mistake for a product to try to please everyone and end up pleasing no one. This process helps prevent that.

- One of the most common mistakes product teams make is confusing themselves with their customers. One thing I really like about personas is that they help shine a light on this all too prevalent problem.

- Many products have many types of users—different types of end-users, managers, administrators, etc., and it's easy to think that you should just put some features in for each of these people, and again, you can end up with a muddled mess. This is partly a design problem, but personas often help you prioritize the importance of these different users, and also realize where you need a separate user experience.

- Personas are a very useful tool for describing to your entire product team who the product is for, how they will use it, and why they will care.

- More generally, much like the product principles, personas have the benefit of rallying the team around a common vision. There are literally thousands of details that will have to be addressed in the course of a product release. The product manager (or designer) can't possibly make every one. If every manager, designer, writer, developer, and tester has taken the product principles and personas to heart, then when faced with an open question, they are more likely to make the right call.

These are some pretty great benefits. But there are also some pitfalls to watch out for:

- Some teams create personas but they don't take the next step—to make the hard choices about which persona should be the priority. It's not ok to say your product is for everyone— you're only deluding yourself. While this is extremely difficult for most product managers, I try hard to get the product manager to focus each release on a single primary persona. It's not that the release won't be valuable and usable by others, but your focus on each release should be to do a great job for just one type of target user.

- Sometimes teams create personas based on their assumptions and stereotypes of their users, and they don't actually take the time to talk to real users and verify if these theorctical people really exist. I have been surprised many times—so many times in fact that I have learned to consider my initial impressions as just a theory, and hold off on real judgments until after talking with real users. In no way is the process of creating a persona a substitute for talking face-to-face with real target users, and testing your designs on real users.

- One question that often comes up is—as you recruit users for your prototype testing—do you only test with users from your primary persona? Certainly you need to make sure your product is great for the people it is intended for, however, you'll want to test with some people from outside this persona as well, as you won't have the luxury of having only primary personas using your product. So for prototype testing, you'll want to recruit a range of possible users.

Examples

You can see example personas at www.svpg.com/examples.

Chapter 18:
REINVENTING THE PRODUCT SPEC

R.I.P. PRD

I think the product spec is long overdue for a renovation. Some would argue that *Agile* methods accomplish this by doing away with the spec altogether. While there are other issues with that, in many respects I think they are on the right track.

But before we get ahead of ourselves, let's start by discussing the problem with today's paper-based specs.

There is of course tremendous range among product specs, starting with what we call them (Product Requirements/PRDs, Market Requirements/MRDs, Business Requirements/BRDs, Functional Specs/FS, and more). The topics covered can vary greatly (these different documents were not intended to serve the same purposes, but over time they have merged and morphed and lost many of their original distinctions), the level of detail, and of course the quality of the spec itself. Even the form varies greatly—many use MS Word documents, but some use spreadsheets, some post the spec on a Wiki site, and others use one of the commercial requirements management tools.

I have seen a few truly good product specs, but most specs take too long to write, they are seldom read, and they don't provide the necessary detail, don't address the difficult questions, nor contain the critical information they need to. And—most important—it is all too easy for the mere existence of the spec to serve as a false indicator to management and the product team that everything is proceeding just fine.

If you agree with me that the central responsibility of the product manager is to make sure that you deliver to the engineering team a product spec that describes a product that will be successful, then we have to acknowledge the weaknesses in the typical spec process and take a hard look at how products are defined.

Here are what I consider the requirements for a good and useful product spec:

- The spec must describe the full user experience—not just the product requirements but also the user interaction and visual design. By now, hopefully everyone recognizes how closely intertwined the requirements are with the user experience design.

- The spec must accurately represent the behavior of the software—and we need to acknowledge that words and pretty pictures are just too limited in their ability to describe this behavior.

- There are several critical consumers of the spec— engineering, QA, customer service, marketing, site operations, sales, and executives. As such, the spec needs to communicate the behavior of the product in a way that all these groups get what they need.

- The spec will change—the rate of change should slow down dramatically once engineering gets started, but there will be decisions and issues that arise, and the spec should change to reflect the very latest decisions.

- There are a number of artifacts in the creation of a spec, such as lists of prioritized requirements, wireframes, and mock-ups, but there needs to be a single master representation of the spec to minimize confusion, ambiguity and versionitis.

In my mind, there's only one form of spec that can deliver on these requirements, and that is the high-fidelity prototype.

The term "high-fidelity" refers to the fact that this should be a realistic representation of the proposed user experience. Except for the most trivial of user interfaces, I am not a fan of so-called paper prototypes. With the tools available today, it is now so quick, easy, and inexpensive to create a high-fidelity prototype for most products that there is no reason not to do so. This is still a prototype, so it's fine to fake (simulate) the backend processing and data, so long as the user experience is plausible.

Over the past few years, my own thinking has evolved here from just prototyping a few critical components of the user experience, to now I advocate prototyping virtually everything—all pages/screens, and all the major use cases. There will still be some error conditions and corner cases that don't pay to prototype, but the benefits of having a high-fidelity representation of the product that the full product team can interact with to understand the product to be built are so great that they dwarf the incremental costs.

It is true that you will still need to supplement the prototype, as there are aspects of the proposed product's behavior that are not easily represented in a prototype, such as business logic (e.g. tax tables and shipping charges), the release requirements (e.g. reliability, performance, scalability) or platform delivery requirements (such as installation requirements, or the list of browser versions to be supported). Also useful as a supplement are use cases, describing the most important flows through the product.

There is still the question of how to best represent this supplementary material. What I really want is to annotate the prototype, but until that technology is readily available, I prefer using a Wiki or other form of Intranet site. The biggest reason is that everyone on the product team knows where to find the latest answers at any time, rather than having various random versions of documents floating around. It is also easy to post questions and answers, set up automatic e-mail notifications whenever the spec is updated, and track the history of decisions.

But the majority of the product spec should be the high-fidelity prototype, representing the functional requirements, the information architecture, the interaction design, and the visual design of the user experience.

In addition to meeting the requirements described above, the most important benefit in my view is that—unlike a paper document—a high-fidelity prototype can be tested. You can put it in front of actual target users and ensure that they can figure out how to use your product (usability), and also determine if they care to use your product (value). You don't actually have a spec worth handing over to engineering until your prototype passes these two tests. Doing this form of testing while you are in QA or Beta is far too late in the process.

I can promise that if you give this a try—creating a high-fidelity prototype of the proposed functionality and user experience—your product team will absolutely love it. Engineers are the immediate winners as they finally get a spec that effectively and unambiguously describes the product they need to build, and that they can refer to at any time when they're confused about how something is supposed to behave. The job of QA is similarly made easier as they now know what should happen when they test the actual product. Marketing, sales, and customer support will love being able to learn the product much earlier in the cycle. You'll also find that your execs will love it too as they can describe what you're doing (and demo the prototype) to investors, board members, and partners much more effectively than any PowerPoint deck can do.

But wait, there's more.

The biggest surprise for most teams is that creating a spec this way will typically significantly reduce time to market. Yep. I realize this may sound counter-intuitive, but to understand why the total time to market is faster, you have to look a little deeper at what almost always happens in a software project. Because the typical spec is so poor (incomplete, ambiguous, and especially untested), and so few of the hard questions and critical details are actually addressed and resolved, it is during the engineering phase that the team is forced to tackle these issues. This results in either tremendous churn (the specs keep changing resulting in delays and frustration in engineering), or the engineers just make assumptions as best they can, and the product that ships is a mess and one or more update releases are required before you actually get something useful to your customers. In either case, the time to market is longer than it should be.

So I truly hope on your next product you'll try this out. Rather than spending weeks working on a 50-page Word document that few will read and is impossible to test, work with your designer to create a prototype of the product you are proposing. Then show that prototype to target users, as well as your product team. You'll end up iterating several times (better now than after engineering spends months building a bad product!), but when you get the recipe right, use that prototype as the basis for the spec you deliver to engineering—and see what happens.

 Examples

You can see example high-fidelity prototypes, and product specs at www.svpg.com/examples.

Chapter 19:

DESIGN VS. IMPLEMENTATION

Define The User Experience Before Proceeding To Build

There are many things in the software development process that can and should be done in parallel. For example, I have long argued that requirements (functionality) and design (user experience design) are intertwined and should be done together. I don't like the old waterfall model of a product manager doing "requirements" and handing that off to interaction designers that do "design." Most teams understand now that this is an obsolete view of product development.

I also believe that great strides have been made by software engineering teams that have learned the value of doing implementation and testing in parallel. The old model of the engineer writing software and then handing it all off to a QA person to test actually takes longer and the result is less reliable. *Agile* methods like *XP* demonstrate the value of doing implementation and testing in concert.

That said, one thing that many teams try to do in parallel—but should not—is user experience design and implementation.

There are several reasons for this:

First, there is a dynamic in software teams that is important to recognize: once implementation begins, it becomes increasingly difficult to make the fundamental changes that will likely be necessary as you work through your user experience design ideas. Partly this is technical—engineering teams must make some early architectural decisions based on assumptions about the requirements and designs in order to make progress. These early decisions are important and have big consequences. Partly, this is psychological—there is a mindset that takes hold once the team shifts into implementation mode, and it's demotivating to go backwards. Partly, this is practical—the clock is ticking, and rework and churn just compounds the pressure the team is under. So even though methods like *Agile* advocate embracing change, you quickly find that some changes are much more welcome than others.

Second, user experience design deals with very difficult questions of both usability and value and, in order to come up with a product that is both usable and valuable, you will need to try ideas out—early and often. One common response is "We'll get feedback during beta," or with *Agile* teams, "We'll test the idea out at the end of the sprint." Unfortunately, this is far too long to wait to test out an idea. A good user experience designer will want to try out dozens of ideas and approaches in a matter of days, and the thought of waiting even for a two- to four-week sprint would be debilitating as the frequency is an order of magnitude too slow.

Third, and related to the above, I argue that to try out an idea you need a high-fidelity prototype. Some will argue that the beta release can be viewed as the prototype, or that the result of the sprint can be viewed as the prototype. But even beyond waiting too long for that software to be available for test, it's important to realize that prototype software is far different than production software. Prototype software needs to be truly disposable. It needs to be something that can be changed substantially in a few hours. What is necessary for production software is like dragging around a boat anchor for a prototype. You'll also find that different types of people like to write prototype versus production software.

Fourth, while it often makes excellent sense to break up a release into several iterations to implement (this reduces risk, improves quality, and eases integration) a user experience is often not something that can be designed in pieces. You have to look at the user experience holistically—it has to make sense to the user at each release. While it's easy to "stub out" software that's not yet available, it's not so easy to do the same for the user experience.

Finally, user experience designers don't necessarily require a lot of time (just as with software engineering, it depends on the methodology they are using, the particular product requirements, and the skills and experience of the specific people), but they do require some time. Even if it's only a week or two.

If you try to start implementation at the same time as design, here's what you will almost certainly see: the designers will be stressed trying to accomplish weeks worth of work in just days, the engineers get anxious as they wait for the designers to give them something, soon the designers will reluctantly make some preliminary guesses to allow the engineers to get going and then hurry to try to get something decent put together before the engineers get too far down the path. However, when they finally do have something, it'll be too late and the engineers will say "we can get to it in the next round" but of course the next round has its own priorities. The designers do not feel good about what is built and shipped, and the customers don't like the result either.

In the worst-case situation, the designers come to the conclusion that they need to go work for a company that prioritizes the user experience.

Fortunately, this really isn't a hard problem to solve. The key is that the user experience design needs to happen before the implementation begins. This is one situation where sequential is important. The requirements and design happen together, and then implementation and test can happen together.

For *Agile* teams, the product manager and user experience designers use the "sprint zero" concept to stay a step or two ahead of the engineers. You are still working to design in as small of increments as possible. It requires a somewhat richer definition of what's in the backlog, but the team will be happier and the product will be better for it.

The exception to the rule is when the engineers have a lot of backend infrastructure work to do. In this situation, the engineering team can be working on this while the user experience is being defined. There will be some interdependencies, but they can be managed. If your user experience designers are about to revolt, have your engineers work on the infrastructure for a release cycle or two, as this gives the designers time to work on creating a backlog of good design.

Note that although I'm advocating that requirements and design are both done before implementation begins, you will still need at least someone from engineering to review the design work from the start, as it's critical for them to assess feasibility and costs along the way. This is necessary to inform the design process. Remember that the objective is to ensure that you discover a product definition that is valuable, and usable.

There is a remarkable amount of confusion out there today in terms of incorporating good design, especially as many teams experiment with *Agile* methods. I think this is unfortunate as with only a few caveats and adjustments, the *Agile* methods can be a huge step forward for teams that previously used conventional waterfall methods. I talk about the root causes of this confusion and how you can get the best of both worlds in the chapter *Succeeding with Agile Methods*.

Chapter 20:
MINIMAL PRODUCT

Cutting Features Versus Slipping Dates

Have you seen this movie before? The one where the product manager comes up with this great product spec that is packed with features—all clearly marked as P1/Must Have, P2/High Want, or P3/Nice to Have. Then he hands the spec off to engineering, and they estimate the costs of the various features, lay the features out against their staff availability, and come up with a schedule that's typically months longer than the product manager needs. So then the negotiating game starts—arguing estimates, cutting features, minimizing QA and beta times, trying to hire some extra contract staff, etc.—all while the clock is ticking.

I'm sure you know the story—even if you haven't seen the movie, you can guess the ending. The product that eventually ships is far from a coherent whole; and no one is happy with it—not the product manager, not the engineers, and definitely not the end users.

Many teams think this is just how the game is played. But this is really just the natural consequence of a flawed process.

Instead, I argue for a very different model:

First, the job of the product manager, working with his designer, is to come up with a high-fidelity prototype with the *minimal functionality necessary* to meet the business objectives, yet with a user experience that users can figure out how to use—and actually want to use. The reason it's so important that the team come up with the minimal functionality is to minimize implementation time and user complexity.

Second, starting at the very beginning of this design process, someone from the engineering team (typically an architect or lead engineer) needs to participate in reviewing the product ideas expressed in the prototype, so she can help the product manager and designer understand the relative and absolute costs of the various product ideas. She can point out any dangerous directions the product might be heading in, or she can go investigate any areas she's unsure about. But by the time the prototype is ready, this engineer must have provided detailed estimates of the surviving features. So the many trade-offs of what is in and what's cut have already been made—and made collaboratively—and at this point the engineering team must have a detailed estimate that they can commit to.

Third, it's essential that this prototype be validated (tested) with real target users. Before committing the resources of the full product team, the product manager and designer must be confident they have come up with something that will succeed. It's not enough to just believe the product definition is good, you have to test to make sure. Just as you wouldn't allow an engineer to ship code just because he or she believed it was good, you must test that code to make sure.

This is why once you've come up with this minimal product—and have tested it with target users to the point that you have evidence it will work—you can't later just cut out some more features and assume it will still work with users. If you could, then you didn't really identify the minimal product earlier.

You will still have some cases where you have the same tough decision—a common situation is when one or more features takes engineering longer to build than they anticipated—but in this model, the normal response is a schedule slip rather than a feature cut. Remember, you've already done the cutting. The good news is that the estimates in this process are better than normal because—with a high-fidelity prototype on which to base an estimate, rather than a paper document—engineering had more time to evaluate the functionality, they feel more ownership in their estimates, and there is also less product to build. So, when slips do occur, they're not as severe or frequent as we are used to.

Similarly, for essentially the same reasons, once the engineering is underway, the product manager can't just keep tossing in additional requirements. By far the most common reason product managers request changes to the spec is a consequence of not really thinking through the requirements in the first place. The high-fidelity prototype will force most of these issues to the surface much earlier in the process.

Some people think that *Agile* methods such as *Scrum* address these issues, but in a different way. While I would love it if most teams switched to *Agile* methods tomorrow, as they really can make a positive difference, you'll find they don't really address these issues, and they create a couple of their own as well. More about that in the chapter *Succeeding with Agile Methods.*

So by all means prioritize as you're thinking about the requirements and what's most important, but by the time you come up with your final spec, make sure your product is already the minimal possible. Then yank all those P1/P2/P3 annotations from the spec, and make it clear to the team that it describes an entire product. And if you remove a leg, then as an old boss of mine would say, that dog won't hunt.

Chapter 21:
PRODUCT VALIDATION

Evidence of Valuable, Usable And Feasible

The past few chapters have had references to what I call product validation. This refers to verifying that the product spec is describing a product that you have *evidence* will be successful, but doing so without actually building out and deploying the product.

This used to be a very expensive and difficult thing to do, and was generally only done for products that were very expensive to tool and manufacture, such as automobiles. However, for just about every type of product today, the costs to produce effective prototypes or simulations has come down so far that I am amazed I continue to encounter product teams that don't do this.

One of the biggest and most common mistakes product teams make is to have far more confidence in their product specifications than they should. They move forward, thinking they'll adjust the product—if necessary—once they get beta feedback. But of course beta is far past the time for major changes, and it is little wonder so many initial product releases are so far off the mark.

As product manager, it is your responsibility to ensure that this doesn't happen to your product. The key is to prove to yourself and to the rest of the product team that the spec you give them describes a winning product. You can do this, and it costs far less than you probably think.

There are three important types of validation that you need to perform before you hand over a final product specification to the engineering team:

Feasibility Testing

One immediate question is whether or not the product is going to be buildable, with the technology time and funds currently available. Your engineers and architects should be very involved in investigating technologies and exploring possible approaches. Some paths will be dead ends, but hopefully others will prove viable.

What is most important is that, if there are obstacles the engineering team considers insurmountable in this product's timeframe, it is important to know this now rather than much later in the process— after the time and money has been lost.

Some products have more technical risks than others, but if yours has significant risks regarding feasibility, make sure you address them early.

Usability Testing

Your interaction designers will be working very closely with you to come up with ways of presenting the functionality in the product so that users can figure out how to use it.

Usability testing will often uncover missing product requirements and, also—if done well—identify product requirements that are not as necessary as originally thought. You should plan on multiple iterations before you come up with a successful user experience.

The purpose of the prototype is to have something to test on real people, and usability testing is the art and science of getting useful feedback on your product from your target customers. Certainly, the product manager and designers will use the prototype and learn a great deal from it, but there is no substitute for putting the prototype in front of real people from the target customer base.

Note that for usability testing purposes, it is perfectly fine if complicated back-end processing is simulated—the key is to evaluate the user experience.

Value Testing

Finally, it is not enough to know that your product is feasible to build and will be usable. What really matters is whether or not your product is something users will find *valuable* and want to buy—that is, how much do users and customers like and value what you're doing?

This testing can typically be combined with the usability testing process, and the prototypes used are the same. But in usability testing, you're seeing if users can figure out how to do the necessary tasks, while in value testing you're seeing if they actually care about those tasks and how well you've solved them.

For a few small product efforts, simply working your ideas out on paper may be sufficient. But for most products—with complex user interactions or new uses of technology—prototypes are absolutely critical in order to assess whether or not the product will meet its objectives.

Most often the prototype is simply quickly assembled and clickable pages representing the eventual web site or software service. But for other types of products the prototype may be a physical device or a combination of device and software. The key is that it needs to be realistic enough that you can test the prototype on actual target customers and they can give you useful feedback.

Until recently, there was debate over the relative merits of "high-fidelity" prototypes (what I'm describing), versus "low-fidelity" prototypes (essentially paper drawings). Today, I consider this debate meaningless because the cost of high-fidelity prototypes has dropped so low, and the quality of the feedback is so much higher.

In the past, there were two major obstacles to these prototyping approaches. The lack of good prototyping tools meant that it could take a long time to construct the prototype. Another problem was in unenlightened management not understanding the difference between a prototype and the real product. Here, teams would be pressured to use the prototype as the basis for the final product, with predictable results in the quality of the implementation.

Today, there are outstanding prototyping tools that can let engineers or designers rapidly create very functional prototypes (often in hours or days) that can effectively emulate the future product—to the degree necessary—and form the basis of realistic user testing. Moreover, most managers today understand that building a simulation and building the actual product are very different animals—akin to building a scale model of a house versus building the actual home.

These are not the only ways to validate your product—especially for Internet services, there are other techniques that are also easy and effective. But I can't emphasize enough how important and valuable it is to validate your ideas before you actually go and build the product. There are always surprises, and it is far better to discover them early rather than when the product is in beta or released. Further, once the real engineering begins, a special type of inertia sets in—it becomes very difficult to make significant changes and the costs of these changes rise dramatically.

In the chapter *Prototype Testing*, I explain in detail the techniques for the usability and value testing.

 Examples

You can see example high-fidelity prototypes, and a list of tools for creating them, at www.svpg.com/examples.

Chapter 22:

PROTOTYPE TESTING

Putting Your Ideas In Front Of Real Users

By this point you should know that I view the high-fidelity prototype as the primary means of describing the product to be built—a prototype is significantly more useful to the product team than the typical paper-based specification. However, that's really the secondary benefit. The primary reason to create a high-fidelity prototype is to help you gain a much deeper understanding of your product, and—ultimately—so that you can test your ideas with real users before you have your engineering teams take months to go build something that you have no real evidence will serve its purpose.

In this chapter I describe how to do this prototype testing. I'll warn you up front that this chapter is relatively long, but I will also say that *testing your ideas with real users is probably the single most important activity in your job as product manager.*

If your company is large enough to have its own usability testing team, by all means secure as much of their time for your project as you can. Even if you can't get much of their time, these people are terrific resources and, if you can make a friend in user research or usability testing, it'll be a huge help to you.

If your organization has funds earmarked for outside services, you may be able to use one of many excellent firms to conduct testing for you. But at US$10,000-$20,000 per round of testing (typically around 10 users) that most of these firms charge, chances are that you won't be able to afford as much testing as your product will need.

If you're like most companies, you have few resources available, and even less money. But you can't let that stop you. It is absolutely essential that you test your ideas out with real users. As I said above, it is arguably the single most important part of your job.

So I'll show you how to do this testing yourself. Don't get me wrong, you won't be as proficient as a trained usability engineer, and it'll take you a few sessions to get the hang of it. But in most cases you'll find that you can still identify the serious issues with your product, which is what's important.

One thing to note is that, while usability testing (seeing if people can figure out how to actually use your product) is critical, you also need to test the value or usefulness of your product (do people actually want to use it?), and we'll discuss both forms of testing here.

Finding Test Subjects

Before you do the prototype testing, you'll need to round up some test subjects. If you're using a lab they'll recruit and schedule the users for you, which is a big help, but if you're on your own, you've got several options:

- If you've established a charter customer program as I described in *Charter User Programs*, you should have quite a few users readily available. If you haven't yet established your program, then you should.

- If you're doing a product for business, then trade shows are a great source of target customers.

- It's increasingly common to advertise for test subjects on *Craigslist*. If you do this, try to keep your participant description a notch more general than specific, and then when you call interested test subjects to explore their participation you can screen for the right match.

- For consumer products you can use your "friends and family" network, but try to avoid people too close to you, and those in the tech industry, unless that's specifically your target. Be sure to use subjects from outside this network, too.

- If you have a list of user e-mail addresses, you can do a selection from there. Often your marketing team can help you narrow down the list.

- You can solicit volunteers on your Web site—lots of major sites do this now. Remember: you'll still call and screen the people to make sure you don't get a sample skewed with early adopter types.

- One technique I especially like for medium to larger companies is to set up regular prototype test sessions—say every other Friday—where you arrange for 10-20 or so users to come into your offices for a couple hours each. Your product managers sign up for the time slots, so a given user might test a couple prototypes each. I like this because one person can do the logistics of invites and screening, and product teams can count on a ready set of test users on a steady basis.

- You can always take your show on the road and go to where your users congregate. If you're doing an e-commerce product, you may want to go to a shopping mall. If you're doing a sports product, go to a sports bar. If your product addresses a real need, you won't have trouble getting people to give you an hour of their time. Just bring some thank you gifts, and try not to look like you're trying to convert their religion.

- If you're asking users to come to your location—especially for business use—you will likely need to compensate the people for their time. If you're doing a consumer service product, a big sincere thank-you along with a hat with your company logo on it will often suffice, as people genuinely want to help in the creation of products—especially for companies they like. However, if you do compensate test subjects, consider providing something along the lines of US$50 of credit on your site.

- Realize that there's a very high no-show rate when you schedule people to come in for testing—it's just a fact of life. While this number can rise to as high as 30%, you can drop it to the 5-10% range by giving your subjects a personal phone call the day before. Even leaving a voicemail message will help, but note that sending an email message does not work equally well.

Preparing the Test

You'll need to define the usability tasks you'll want to test, and the interview questions concerning value:

- Define in advance the set of tasks you want to test. Usually these tasks are fairly obvious. If you're building an e-mail client, for example, your users will need to do things such as compose a message, read new mail, and file away messages. There will also be more obscure tasks, but concentrate on the primary tasks—the ones that users will do most of the time. If you have time, you can get to less common tasks but it's essential the key tasks are tested well.

- You have a one-time-only opportunity with each user you test—the opportunity to learn how they think about this problem today, without your product. If you're testing a new online restaurant rating service, rather than start them out at your prototype's home page, you might instead want to start them out with an empty browser and see what they do. What review sites do they use today? Do they use Google or Yahoo's search to find the specific restaurant, or do they go somewhere like OpenTable or Zagat? Do they search by neighborhood, by cuisine type, or price range? This type of incredibly valuable information is missed if you jump right into your prototype, which will necessarily have quite a few assumptions built in. Once your test subjects have the opportunity to play with your prototype for a while, they can tell you what they like better, but they will no longer be thinking about the problem the way a first-time visitor would.

- You'll then want to get them to your prototype, but there's one more thing before you jump into your tasks. See if they can tell from the home page or landing page of your prototype what it is that you actually do, and especially what might be valuable or appealing to them. Again, once they jump into tasks, they'll lose that first-time visitor context, so don't waste the opportunity. You'll find that landing pages are incredibly important to bridging the gap between expectations and what the site actually does.

- After you've seen if your user can figure out how to do the tasks you're testing, now is the right time to have a conversation with him or her. Think of it as a one-person focus group. Does the person use a different product or site for the same purpose today, or is this something they do manually or offline? How much better is this than what they use today? And don't forget to ask my favorite question, Net Promoter Score (NPS): How likely would you be to recommend this product to your friends? Now that the user has interacted with your prototype, they understand the topic and you can have an extremely useful dialogue with them about this problem. Most importantly, you're trying to gauge how much this person values the product.

- It's useful if you structure your questions on a scale, such as 0-10, or with numeric answers in general. This is so that you can track the averages as they improve. One technique I like for gauging value is to ask how much the user would be willing to pay for it, even if you have no intention of actually charging for use this way. It's a way to assess value and—especially—to track how the average value goes up or down over time as you change the prototype.

- Note that you don't have to wait until you have a complete prototype in order to begin testing. You can start with the main tasks, and it's okay if you have dead ends in the rest of the prototype. If the user wanders over to one of those dead ends, just ask "And what would you expect to happen if you did that?" This is a great question whether you have that path laid out or not. If you do have it laid out, you can see if they match. And if you don't, you'll get important info about what you'll need to do.

The Test Environment

Here's how to prepare your test environment:

- Formal testing labs will typically have setups with two-way mirrors or closed-circuit video monitors, as well as cameras that capture both the screen and a frontal view of the user. Just know that while that's great if you have it, you do not need these things to have an extremely useful and valuable test. I can't count how many prototypes I've tested at a tiny table at Starbucks—just big enough for a laptop—with three chairs around the table. In fact, in some ways this is preferable to the testing lab because the user feels a lot less like a lab rat and may be more candid and open in his or her responses.

- The other environment that works quite well is your customer's office. It may be time consuming to go there and get set up, but even 30 minutes in their office will often tell you a lot. And because they are "master of their domain," they're frequently very open and talkative. Also, all the cues are there in the office to remind them of how they might actually use the product in their daily routine. You can also learn a lot from observing what the office looks like. How big is their monitor? How fast is their computer and network connectivity? How do they communicate with their colleagues on their work tasks?

- There are tools for doing this type of testing remotely, but while you can see where their mouse is, and what the user is clicking on, it's not the same as looking at the person's eyes and body language. So, again, while more testing is generally better, this is not a substitute for face-to-face testing.

- As product manager, you need to make sure you are at every single test—do not delegate this task. Real value comes from experiencing as many users as possible—first hand—interacting with and responding to your ideas. Even if you use an outside firm to arrange and administer the tests, you need to be there with them during the testing. No one knows your product as well as you do, and you will have insights from watching the slightest hesitation or confused look, or the nuance of a question that reveals that your test subjects don't understand the conceptual model or particular feature. What gets summarized for you by a proctor will probably miss several key insights.

- Some people believe that the product manager (and the interaction designer) are too close to the product to do this type of testing objectively—that they may either get their feelings hurt or only hear what they want to hear. My view is that good product managers and interaction designers get past this very quickly. They know they will get the product wrong initially—that almost nobody gets it right the first time—and they know that learning from these tests is the fastest path to an inspiring product. So to me the benefits far outweigh the risks.

- Ideally, you should have one person administer the tests and another person taking notes. It's very useful to have someone to debrief with afterwards to make sure you both saw the same things and came to the same conclusions. That said, if it's just you and your laptop—and you've got a ready and willing target user in front of you—do it. It's all good.

- If you as product manager have a user researcher or usability engineer along with you, let him or her administer the test while you take notes. Otherwise, you'll probably be the one that administers. It's great to invite others on the product team to be your note taker. Most often this person will probably be the interaction designer, but the visual designer, managers, and especially engineers are all useful and they'll get a lot out of the experience.

Testing Your Prototype

Now that you've got your prototype ready, you've lined up your test subjects, and you've prepared the tasks and questions, here are a set of tips and techniques for administering the actual testing:

- Greet the person warmly and offer a coffee or bottle of water, but the sooner you get to the prototype the better. Tell your subject you'll chat with them after they test the prototype, but you want to get their untainted impressions first. The more you chat beforehand, the more clues you are giving away and the less of a true first impression your test subject can provide. If more than five minutes goes by without the user starting in on the prototype you are talking too much.

- After your greeting, be sure to tell him or her that (1) this is just a prototype—it's a very early product idea—and it's not real, (2) they won't be hurting your feelings by giving you their honest opinion—good or bad, and (3) you're testing the prototype—you're not testing him or her. Your test subject can't pass or fail—only the prototype can pass or fail.

- When testing, you'll want to do everything you can to keep your users in "use mode" and out of "critique mode." What matters is whether users can easily do the tasks they need to do, and whether they value the product. It really doesn't matter if the user thinks something on the page is ugly or should be moved or changed. Sometimes misguided testers will ask users questions like "What three things on the page would you change?" To me, unless that user happens to be an interaction designer, I'm not really interested in the answer to that question, or others like it. If users knew what they really wanted, software would be a lot easier to create. So watch what they do more than what they say.

- During the testing, the main skill you have to learn is to keep quiet. Normally, when we see someone struggle, most of us have an urge to help the person out. You need to suppress that urge. You have to turn into a horrible conversationalist and get comfortable with silence.

- There are three important cases you're looking for: (1) the user got through the task with no problem at all and no help, (2) the user struggled and moaned a bit but eventually got through it, or (3) the user got so frustrated he gave up. Sometimes people will give up pretty quick, so you may need to encourage them to keep trying a bit longer. But if the user gets to the point that you believe he would truly leave the site and go to a competitor, then that's when you note he truly gave up.

- In general, you'll want to avoid giving any help or "leading the witness" in any way. If you see the user scrolling the page up and down and clearly looking for something, it's okay to ask the user what specifically he's looking for, as that information is very valuable to you. Some people ask users to keep a running narration of what they're thinking, but I find this tends to put people in critique mode, as it's not a natural behavior.

- Act like a parrot. This helps in many ways. First, it helps avoid leading. If your test subject is quiet and you can't stand it any longer, tell them what they're doing: "I see that you're looking at the list on the right." This will prompt them to tell you what they're trying to do, looking for, whatever. If your subject asks a question, rather than giving a leading answer you can play back the question to them, "Will clicking on this make a new entry?" The subject will usually take it from there because they'll want to answer your question: "Yeah, I think it will." Parroting also helps avoid leading value judgments. If you have the urge to say "Great!," instead say "You created a new entry." Finally, parroting key points also helps your note taker because he or she will have more time to write down important points.

- Fundamentally, you're trying to get an understanding of how your target users think about this problem, and to identify places in your prototype where the model the software presents is inconsistent or incompatible with how the user is thinking about the problem. That's what it means to be counterintuitive. Fortunately, when you spot this it is usually not hard to fix, and can be a big win for your product.

- You will find that you can tell a great deal from body language and tone. It is painfully obvious when test subjects don't like your ideas, and it is also clear when they genuinely do. If they like what they see, they'll almost always ask for an email telling them when the product is out. And if they really like it, they'll try to get access from you before it's released to the general public. When I attend the prototype testing with my clients in Germany, even though I don't speak German, it is obvious what the issues are—which ideas work well and which ones don't.

Updating the Prototype

The point of this prototype testing is to identify what you need to fix in the prototype to make it more valuable and usable. So, as quickly as possible, you'll want to correct the problems.

- Some people believe you have to freeze the prototype, the tasks, and the questions for a complete round of testing (generally 6-8 users) before drawing any conclusions. I don't think that's true. I have found that you can significantly accelerate the process of getting to a good product by responding more quickly to feedback. You don't have to be hit on the head by eight users in a row to know you need to fix something big. So go ahead and fix it when you feel you've identified a problem, even if it's after only two or three users. The harder question is deciding when you're done. Generally, if you can get through six consecutive users who understand and appreciate the value of the product—and can get through the key tasks—you're in good shape and you've done your job.

- You might determine that you just aren't able to get people interested in this problem, or figure out a way to make the product clear or usable enough that your target users realize its value. In this case, you may decide to stop right there and put the idea on the shelf. Some product managers consider this a big failure. I view it as saving the company the wasted cost of building and shipping a losing product, not to mention the opportunity cost of what your engineering team could be building instead.

This whole process might sound complicated or difficult, but the remarkable thing is just how easy and effective it actually is. The best way to prove this to yourself is to take your laptop with your product or prototype on it to someone that hasn't seen it yet and just give it a try.

I want to give credit here to two important sources (and great resources for you).

The first is the book, *Don't Make Me Think* by Steve Krug. It's mostly a book on interaction design, but in the back third he makes a compelling case for this sort of informal testing, and he provides many useful tips. I have long recommended this book to both product managers and designers, and I hope you'll buy a copy and read it carefully.

Second, my favorite product testing firm is Creative Good (www. creativegood.com). These guys specialize in a form of testing they call *Listening Labs*, which is a powerful form of undirected testing that can find huge issues with your product—functionality and design—resulting in dramatic improvements to the business results. While most testing firms test the products on a task basis, these guys are good at looking at the big picture, which is where many of the biggest improvements are to be found. Several of the techniques described above are adapted from their testing methodology.

Chapter 23:

IMPROVING EXISTING PRODUCTS

It's Not About Adding Features

Many product managers get thrown off course when it comes to continuing development on an existing product. Most have a detailed product roadmap with all their great ideas of what they should add, or the roadmap is loaded with requirements that come from specific customers—"If you want me to buy this you'll need to add these six features…"

Most product organizations are essentially feature factories (with some bug fixing thrown in). For them it is all about adding features.

But all too often these added features just end up making the situation worse and not better. I try to get product teams to look at product improvement differently.

As with new product development, everything starts with having a very clear understanding of what you're trying to achieve. For example, let's say you're the product manager responsible for new insurance coverage applications at an online insurance site.

There are all kinds of great metrics for you to track. How many users visit the start of the application process? How many drop off at each page? How many refuse to give personal information? How many confirm their e-mail addresses? How many complete the process?

Let's say that today only 7% of the people who begin the registration process actually complete it. If you can drive that number up to 15%, look what you've just done for your product and your company.

To accomplish this goal, you might find that you need some new features, and the justification for the new feature is the degree to which it can improve these metrics.

It is likely there are elements of the user experience that can be improved. Or maybe you don't need as much personal information from the user at this stage as you think you do. Or maybe you're not being clear enough as to why you require this information. Or perhaps users are not sure they can trust you with this data.

Your job as product manager is to live and breath these metrics. Every day you should ask yourself what you can do to improve them. And you work closely with an interaction designer, user researcher, and lead engineer to consider possibilities.

Your primary tools for gaining insight into what's going on are to study the site analytics, and to test your product on real users. You'll also gather data from NPS tracking, customer service, the sales force, and from win/loss analysis.

This type of product improvement is often extremely rewarding, especially for Internet services because we have so much great data—near real-time data—giving us feedback on our ideas. It's amazing how quickly and how dramatically you can help your business as you act on what you have learned from the data.

Remember that it's not about what a particular customer thinks is important to add, or the result of a survey, or a focus group. What matters is what actually moves the needle on the metrics you are driving towards.

So when you're trying to improve an existing product, don't fall into the trap of gathering subjective feedback, eliciting customer requirements and chasing features. Instead, focus on relentlessly pursuing your metrics by studying live use and working the numbers in the right direction.

 Examples

You can see example prototype testing questions at www.svpg. com/examples.

Chapter 24:
GENTLE DEPLOYMENT

Help Prevent User Abuse

User abuse is when you unnecessarily and (hopefully) unintentionally mistreat your users by releasing changes to the user community that they don't appreciate. I know it's hard to believe that not every one of your users is waiting excitedly for all of your changes, but it's true. There are several reasons why your users may feel this way:

- They may not have received any notice of the changes, so they were caught by surprise—and they weren't in the mood for a surprise.

- They may not have time at the moment to learn the changes and you don't have a way for them to continue to use the old version until they do.

- The new change may not actually work.

- The new change may be incompatible with early versions (such as for accessing data).

- The new change may work but it is perceived as gratuitous.

- They may already be fatigued from all of the changes you have recently made.

- They may have their own layer of process or behavior built around your previous version, and now that is broken and they have to update it.

So what causes user abuse?

Mainly change. As a general rule, users don't like change. Sure they want the software to be great, and they clamor for new functionality, but most people aren't excited about taking the time to learn a new way to do something they can already do.

Of course, that's a problem, as most of us are in the business of change. We have product teams working relentlessly to add value and deliver new capabilities to our users and customers. Needs change, technologies change, markets change— and our software must change along with them.

The solution to user abuse isn't to prevent change, it's to be smart about deploying change.

One of the fun things about working on a 1.0 product is that you get to start fresh with your community of users. It's true that your user base is still influenced by other products and services that they've been exposed to, but overall you don't have to worry much about things like backwards compatibility or retraining your users. However, for most of us, we're in the business of creating updates or new versions of existing products or services.

In the past, software companies could much more easily get away with sending out largely incompatible and disruptive updates. While users would gripe, they weren't as able to influence other potential users around the world, or take their business elsewhere. Today, with the pervasiveness of the Internet—and the free flow of user product reviews, both good and bad—if you turn out a bad release of your product, and you don't correct the problems quickly, you'd better brace yourself for some serious community backlash.

For large-scale consumer Internet services, this is an even more serious concern. These sites need to consider community impact in everything they say and do, beginning with software updates. I call the process of deploying updates intelligently and carefully to a large community of users "gentle deployment."

In the spirit of minimizing the disruption caused by change, there are several techniques that can be useful in deploying changes gently.

First, do everything you can to communicate the changes in advance, through vehicles such as newsletters, onsite education, and tutorials. But remember that many people will have neither the time nor the inclination to read what you write, so this technique can only take you so far.

Second, if there is any question about the new version of your product working properly—either due to reliability issues, or scale, or performance—then you need to redouble your QA efforts to ensure that you won't have to rollback your updates, which compounds community angst significantly.

Third, if the change is significant, it may be important to contain the risk by pursuing some form of gentle deployment such as parallel, or incremental deployment.

You can do this by deploying a parallel version of your product and inviting people to opt-in and try out the new version when they have the time. Allow those who try to use the new version to make it their default if they like it. Once you are confident that the new version is working well—and the majority of your community has converted to using it—you can make it the default and allow customers to "opt-out" and continue to use the old version for a period of time if they don't have the time to learn the changes immediately. Give these people sufficient notice of when support for the old version will be discontinued. For a significant client or service with a large community, expect this process to take months. Also expect some heat from your engineering and site operations organizations because it is not easy to support parallel versions.

Another gentle deployment approach is to deploy regionally—first trying out the new version in a limited area of the country or world, and then expanding. Or you can deploy the changes incrementally—introducing the changes in bite-size pieces over time.

However you choose to go about it, the key is to be as sensitive as possible to the disruption that your changes will cause. Give people the opportunity to learn the differences when they have the time, and try to minimize the impact of any problems or issues your changes may cause.

If your users like your product or service, you've got a reserve of goodwill to draw upon. But save it for when you really need it—don't waste that goodwill through user abuse.

Chapter 26:

RAPID RESPONSE

Finish What You Start And Save Entire Release Cycles

I've discussed elsewhere in this book the pitfalls of confusing product launch with success, and how important it is to not lose focus after you ship your product or service. In this chapter, I take a closer look at what you should be doing during this critical phase of your project.

In many organizations, the resources that have been marshaled to build and launch the product evaporate very quickly after launch so they can be applied to the next project coming along. This is especially unfortunate because this is the moment when your opportunity for learning and correcting is greatest. I consider this a project management and product development process failing that can be corrected simply by slightly extending the project to incorporate this critical phase. No phase of the process will provide a better ROI than this one, so the change is not a difficult pitch to management.

I advocate that all project teams schedule a phase that begins at launch and lasts typically a few days to a week. I call this phase rapid response, to emphasize that it is all about responding quickly to what you learn once the product has been launched.

Note that while this approach was borne out of consumer Internet services where it is particularly critical, I believe it is important for platform, infrastructure, and enterprise products as well.

Even if you've done all of the early prototypes and validation testing prior to engineering that I advocate—and you have a great QA team so the product is reliable—you still need to expect that there will be issues that can only be discovered once you're live. The typical approach of waiting to see what the response is and if any issues exist—and then trying to schedule follow-on point releases following the same general cycle—takes far too long and costs far too much.

The question is not whether there will be issues but, rather, how quickly will you address them?

When measuring success, you need to have a clear, prioritized set of business metrics. Are you looking at page views? Registered users? Time on site? Conversion rates from visitor to member? Subscriptions? Advertising revenue? The right set of metrics will depend on your product and your business goals but, in any case, you need to know what you care about and what you'll be tracking. Further, you need to know what results you would consider to be a success and what results you would consider to be a problem.

For consumer Internet services, it has never been easier to understand how people are using your product or service. It is easy to instrument and track activity—there are many products in this space. Services such as *Google Analytics* (www.google.com/analytics) can quickly and easily tell you a great deal about how your users are using your service.

For enterprise software, I like to send members of the product team—product manager, engineers, designers—out to the customer site to be there with them when they install the software and work to get the software live and in use. It is amazing how much faster issues are identified and resolved when a team member understands she's going to be at the customer site until the customer is live and referenceable.

Once the issues have been identified, the product team (product manager, interaction designer, lead engineers, customer service, marketing, etc.) needs to meet no less than daily, prioritize the issues, and discuss the best way to respond. The result might be a "hot fix" that is rushed to the site, or possibly additional content that explains problem areas. If the team is prepared for these changes— and understands how crucial it is to identify and respond quickly— then, in a very short amount of time, it can make substantial improvements to the effectiveness of the product or service.

Site analytics are not the only tool you should use to understand your users and how they feel about your site. Surveys, e-mail discussions, message boards, and field testing are other examples. But the data provides such near-real-time insights that I look at the Web site analytics for all of the sites that I am involved in nearly daily. I'm very often looking at where people are coming from, what their favorite pages and activities are, how long people are spending on the site, how many pages they are viewing, and how often they return. Customer service, sales, and partners are also good sources of input for rapid response fixes.

Chapter 26:

SUCCEEDING WITH AGILE METHODS

Top 10 List

Many software product teams are either currently experimenting with *Agile* methods, or have recently adopted some form of the methods. While the benefits of *Agile* methods—including *Scrum* and *XP*—are many, most product teams struggle initially as they work to understand how best to apply *Agile* methods which were originally developed for the custom software world to their product software environment.

In this chapter I highlight the keys for succeeding with *Agile* in a *product* software environment.

If you don't yet know what *Agile* methods are, take a look at www.agilemanifesto.org.

Note that this list is meant for product software teams. For custom software, there are some very different considerations.

1. The product manager is the product owner, and he represents the customer. He will need to be extremely involved with the product development team, helping to drive the backlog and especially answer questions as they arise. Some misguided product managers think they get

off easy in an *Agile* environment—they couldn't be more wrong. Some also like to have different people covering the product manager and the product owner role, but this is usually just a symptom of a deeper problem (see the chapter *Product Management vs. Product Marketing*)

2. Using *Agile* is not an excuse for a lack of product planning. As a product manager/owner, you still need to know where you're going, what you're trying to accomplish, and how you'll measure success. That said, in an *Agile* environment, your planning horizon can be somewhat shorter and rolling. You should use the lightweight opportunity assessment instead of a heavy MRD (see the chapter *Opportunity Assessments*).

3. You and your designers should always try and be one or two sprints ahead of your team. This allows you to validate difficult features with sufficient time to improve them. Insist that the designers (interaction designers and visual designers) are front and center in the process, and make sure they don't try to do their design work during the sprint—while the implementation is already underway (see the chapter *Design vs. Implementation*). Make sure, however, that someone from the engineering team is reviewing your ideas and prototypes every step of the way to provide feedback on feasibility, costs, and insights into better solutions.

4. Break the design work into as small and as independent chunks as possible, but not too small—make sure you don't try to design a house one room at a time. But remember the emphasis on coming up with the minimal product possible. Note that, in an *Agile* environment, the designers may need to work faster than they're comfortable with. You'll find that certain designers, and certain design methodologies—such as rapid prototyping—are more compatible with the pace of an *Agile* environment than others.

5. As a product manager/owner, your main responsibility is to come up with valuable and usable prototypes and user stories that your team can build from. Replace heavy PRDs and functional specs with prototypes and user stories. Do prototypes for three reasons: (1) so you can test with real users, (2) to force yourself to think through the issues; and (3) so you have a good way to describe to engineering what you need built during the sprint. Be sure to test prototypes with real users. Try out your ideas and iterate on the prototype until you've got something worth building. You still need to make sure that you don't waste sprint cycles.

6. Let engineering break up the sprints into whatever granularity they prefer. Sometimes the functionality in a prototype can be built in a single sprint, other times it may take several sprints. You will find that having good prototypes will help significantly in estimating the amount of work and time required to build. Remember that the engineering team has considerations in the areas of quality, scalability, and performance, so let them chunk the functionality into sprints as they see fit.

7. Make sure you as product manager/owner and your interaction designer are at every daily status meeting (aka *standup* or daily *scrum*). These morning meetings are the beginning of the communication process, not the end. There will be a constant stream of discussion about the product. Designers should be previewing functionality to the developers and QA. Developers should be showing off completed code to each other, QA, and the designers and product manager. QA and developers should be identifying potential pitfalls during prototyping, and helping the team to make better functionality, design and implementation trade-offs.

8. Don't just launch every sprint—reassemble sprint results in a staging area until you have enough to make a release as defined by the product manager/owner. It's the product

manager's job to ensure that there is sufficient functionality to warrant a release to the user. Remember that in a product environment, constant change can be upsetting to your customers (see the chapter *Gentle Deployment*).

9.   At the end of each sprint, make sure you demo the current state of the product, as well as the prototype for the next sprint. Having everyone see what you finished validates the team's hard work, gives the entire company insight into the product, and keeps the evangelism going.

10. Get *Agile* training for your entire team. Hire a consultant to help your product team move to *Agile*, but make sure the consultant has proven experience with product software teams and understands the difference between product software and IT or custom software. If everyone understands the mechanisms around *Agile*, then you can focus on the execution. If people don't understand, you'll get bogged down in the semantics and dogmatic issues.

 CAN'T EARLY SPRINTS BE CONSIDERED A PROTOTYPE?

Some *Agile* advocates and practitioners argue that the team should just consider the early sprints as the working prototype. And in fact, for custom software efforts where there really isn't true product management and rarely user experience design, this is the essentially the best you can do. However, for product software organizations, you can and must do better than this, for three reasons:

First, a sprint is typically far too long to wait to try out an idea—an idea which will most likely be wrong. It is much faster to try that idea out with a disposable prototype in days rather than wait months for one or more sprint cycles.

Second, there are typically too many critical things for the engineering team to do to use them for the product discovery process. By taking their time for this prototyping work they are not able to do what they should be doing—building production software.

Third, while *Agile* methods do much to encourage the team to learn and respond quickly, it is still difficult and time consuming for a team to change directions significantly once they have begun down a path, and put long hours into a particular architecture or approach.

 ## CAN AGILE BE USED FOR PRODUCT SOFTWARE?

Agile methods like *Scrum* really do attack some key problems that have plagued software teams for decades. But many product managers and user experience designers—and to a lesser extent QA staff—are initially confused by *Agile* and unsure of their role in these methods. To be clear, these methods absolutely require these roles, but I attribute the confusion to the origin of *Agile* methods. I've found that when I explain the origins, it helps to illuminate the problems that *Agile* was designed to solve, and what challenges remain.

Many are surprised to learn that *Scrum*, the most popular of the *Agile* methods, is now over 20 years old. It was created in 1986 in Japan. (Yet another example of just how long it can take for a new idea to reach the tipping point).

But most importantly, these methods originated in the custom software world.

The custom software world—building special purpose software for specific customers—has long been a brutally difficult type of software. This is partly because customers notoriously don't know what they want, but they have a need so they write a contract with a custom software supplier, or sit down with their internal IT folks, who then work to deliver. When they do deliver, the customer invariably responds that it really wasn't what they had in mind, so the cycle repeats and frustration mounts. But the core need still exists, so this provides job security for countless IT developers, custom software shops, and professional services businesses.

Further, custom software has long been on the short end of the stick when it comes to recruiting and retaining top software talent.

This is partly the case because many top software professionals prefer to work for companies that are in the business of creating software for thousands, if not millions of customers. And partly it's because software professionals get paid more working for product software companies where the product team is responsible for coming up with software products that please many people, or they don't make money. So these companies know they must hire the talent necessary to create winning products, and they pay accordingly. But to put this in perspective, only a relatively small percentage of software people actually work on commercial product software—most work on custom software.

In the custom software model, since the customer believes he knows what he needs, you'll rarely find the role of the product manager. Likewise, you'll almost never find user experience designers. The reasons for this are more complex, and involve a degree of ignorance (relatively few in the custom software world realize what user experience designers do and why they're needed), and cost sensitivity (cut costs by letting the developers design). But to be fair—due to the shortage of user experience designers in our industry—the few available are immediately grabbed by the product companies that realize how critical they are, so custom software teams can rarely find designers even if their leaders realize they need them. Similarly, QA as a discipline is rarely found in custom software projects—again, the developers are typically expected to do the required testing.

Another crucial element in understanding the custom software world is that the vast majority of custom software projects are relatively small and done to support the internal operations of a company—applications such as HR, billing, and manufacturing—where the limited number of users means that issues such as scalability and performance are usually less critical.

Historically the custom software world used the Waterfall process because the various stakeholders needed a way to monitor progress during the long process of creating these contract applications. In fact, the Waterfall methods originated here as well.

In the product software world, where the software must sell on its own merits, we introduced the roles of product managers to represent the needs of a wide range of customers, user experience designers to create effective user experiences, and QA testers to ensure the software worked as advertised in the range of customer environments.

But in the custom software world, the same fundamental issues of coming up with something that satisfied the customer continued.

For these teams, especially, the *Agile* methods represent significant improvements. They improve communication between the customer and the engineers. They significantly reduce the risk by building smaller, more frequent iterations so that the customer can learn whether he really likes something or not much sooner—rather than waiting for the end of a long process. They help introduce some modern software testing concepts, and they help relieve the team from spending countless hours preparing documents that are rarely read—and quickly obsolete.

In general, these are great benefits for product software teams as well, but I always explain that a few adjustments are required. I've written earlier about these topics—such as how to insert user experience design into the process, and how to manage releases and deployments—but another area that has struggled is architectural design.

Agile methods encourage engineers to not get attached to their implementation, believing that things can be re-factored or re-architected relatively quickly and easily. This is true for the vast majority of custom software, but for many product software systems, such as large-scale consumer Internet services—which must support hundreds of thousands if not millions of users—this approach can be naïve.

So it shouldn't be a big surprise that the main issues many product software teams encounter with *Agile* methods stem from their custom software origin. Many *Agile* books, articles, and training classes still don't mention product managers—or any form of user experience designers (interaction designers and visual designers)—because they aren't meant for product software teams.

My suggestion to teams moving to *Agile* is to make sure the firm you hire to help your organization transition to *Agile* actually understands the differences that product software demands. Most don't, but some do.

Chapter 27:

SUCCEEDING WITH WATERFALL PROCESSES

Proactively Addressing The Issues

In this chapter we look at the Waterfall process—the product development process that the majority of product teams still follow.

Even though the Waterfall development process is more than 30 years old—and even though it is often cursed by engineers and product managers alike, including me—it is still the most common process used to create software products.

While it has long been unfashionable for a team to describe their product development process as waterfall, in most cases that is essentially what is still being followed, albeit by many different names including: *Successive Refinement, SDLC, Phase-Gate, Stage Review, Staged Contracts, and Milestone-based.*

In this chapter we'll explore the key weaknesses of this approach but, most importantly, we'll discuss what the product manager must do in order to maximize the chance of success with this process.

General Principles

The conventional waterfall process is extremely simple in concept:

1. **Phased development.** Software progresses through a well-

defined series of phases, including: a written description of the requirements, user experience design, high-level architectural design, low-level detailed design, code, testing, and deployment.

2. **Phase review.** Each phase ends with a review of the deliverables from that phase, followed by sign-off and an explicit transition to the next phase.

The Waterfall method can be applied either informally or very formally, as in the US Department of Defense Standard 2167A (and later 498), which describes in excruciating detail every step of the process along with the many document deliverables.

Similarly, the Waterfall method is also at the heart of the following very informal and much more common scenario: Someone from the marketing department gathers some market requirements and delivers them to engineering, which comes up with a schedule and works on an architectural design, and then some detailed designs for the more complicated areas. The product then moves into implementation and testing, often a beta, and finally deployment.

While we will soon discuss the most serious limitations of this approach, it is also useful to acknowledge the key traits that have kept this process in use for so long:

- Management appreciates the (perceived) predictability of the process. It is possible, although not common, to come up with fairly accurate schedules for even large and complex software projects. This assumes, however, that you completely and accurately understand the requirements and the technology, and that there will be no changes. With iterative approaches, you don't really know how many iterations will be required, and this can be disconcerting to management.
- There are deliverables throughout the process. Many people (managers, customers/clients, and even some engineers)

are reassured by seeing well thought-out and thorough documents and design diagrams. It helps these people to gauge progress towards the end, and it also helps them feel better about the level of thinking that has gone into the project (even though there is no way to test whether or not the confidence is justified because unlike software you can't execute paper documents). Many people make the mistake of feeling unjustifiably reassured by impressive specifications and documents.

Product Management Concerns

There are a number of well-known concerns with this process, especially from the product manager's perspective:

Validation Occurs Too Late in the Process

The most costly issue is that there is typically no actual working software until nearly the end of the process, so there is little if any visibility into whether the software will be useful until after the majority of the investment has been made.

The product manager must ensure that, prior to moving into the expensive design and implementation phases, the product must be prototyped and tested on actual target users. This ensures the specification that is eventually provided to the product development organization describes a product that has been successfully validated with the target audience.

Likewise, if there are major technical risks, these too should be explored and feasibility questions resolved (by the engineering organization) prior to beginning the actual architectural design and implementation. Before proceeding, the team needs to know that the product specification is something that can be successfully delivered.

Changes Are Costly and Disruptive

Any change to decisions from previous stages destabilizes the process and causes considerable pain and cost, as much work has to be reviewed and reworked. Moreover, the coding and testing process often uncovers issues in requirements and in architecture that can cause major delays and pain in this process.

The product manager must constantly represent the voice of the customer and user and there will be times when changes are required. It is important to point out that the cost of postponing the change needs to include the cost of the follow-on release to make the correction. There will still be times when it makes the most sense to defer the change until the next release, but in many cases it will be less expensive to course correct sooner rather than later.

Responding to the Market

This approach has a relatively high overhead in terms of documentation and process for moving through the phases. One consequence of this is that it can take considerable time to make even relatively small changes to the software.

This puts additional pressure on the product manager to ensure that they are providing a validated specification for a successful product in the first place, but it also means that the product manager will need to work with the product team to make course corrections as quickly as possible after release.

Summary

We have all seen the consequences of the Waterfall process in practice, and it's not hard to understand the motivation for alternatives such as the *Agile* methods *Scrum* and *XP*.

In many ways, the Waterfall process represents an idealistic but naïve view of the software development process, where people are able to anticipate the key issues and fully understand the requirements. When this is the case—usually only for very small projects—this approach can provide a reasonable path to a quality implementation.

Unfortunately, this is rarely the case with product software. In practice, the consequence is that the product ships later than planned due to changes, and then expensive, time-consuming follow-on releases are required to correct issues once real users have a chance to see and use the software.

That said, the product development process is often deeply entrenched in the product development organization, and the best the product manager can do is to ensure that potential problems are avoided. The most important thing is to ensure that during the requirements and design phases, the emphasis must be on true product discovery – identifying a product that is valuable, usable and feasible – and that the product spec is validated (by building a prototype and testing it with real users) prior to moving to the implementation phase. If you do this, you'll not only stand a much better chance of defining an inspiring and successful product, but you'll also save your team significant time and cost.

Chapter 28:
STARTUP PRODUCT MANAGEMENT

It's All About Product Discovery

I've been working with quite a few startups over the past few years—usually in an advisory capacity, but sometimes more directly involved. Startups are essentially all about new product creation, so they're a terrific place for product managers to do their thing, and it's why I love working with startups so much. Yet I believe that the prevalent model for how startups come up with their first product is terribly inefficient, and it's why so many otherwise good ideas never get funded or make it to market.

Here's how the model typically works: Someone with an idea gets some seed funding, and the first thing he does is hire some engineers to start building something. The founder will have definite ideas on what she wants, and she'll typically act as product manager and often product designer, and the engineering team will then go from there. The company is typically operating in "stealth mode" so there's little customer interaction. It takes much longer than originally thought for the engineering team to build something, because the requirements and the design are being figured out on the fly.

After six months or so, the engineers have things in sort of an alpha or beta state, and that's when they first show the product around. This first viewing rarely goes well, and the team starts scrambling. The run rate is high because there's now an engineering team building this thing as fast as they can, so the money is running out and the product isn't yet there. Maybe the company gets additional funding and a chance to get the product right, but often it doesn't. Many startups try to get more time by outsourcing the engineering to a low-cost off-shore firm, but they're still left with the same process and the same problems.

Here's a very different approach to new product creation, one that costs dramatically less and is much more likely to yield the results you want: The founder hires a product manager, an interaction designer, and a prototyper. Sometimes the designer can also serve as prototyper, and sometimes the founder can serve as the product manager, but one way or another, you have these three functions lined up—product management, interaction design, and prototyping— and the team starts a process of very rapid product discovery.

I describe this process in detail in the chapter *Reinventing the Product Spec*, but there are two keys:

1. The idea is to create a high-fidelity prototype that mimics the eventual user experience

2. You need to validate this product design with real target users.

In this model, it's normal to create literally dozens of versions of the prototype—it will evolve daily, sometimes with minor refinements and sometimes with very significant changes. But the point is that with each iteration you are getting closer to identifying a winning product.

This process typically takes between a few weeks and a few months. At the end of the process, you have (a) identified a product that you have validated with the target market, (b) a very rich prototype that serves as a living spec for the engineering team to build from, and (c) a much greater understanding of what you're getting into, and what you'll need to do to succeed.

Now, when you bring on an engineering team, they'll start off with a tremendous advantage—a clear understanding of the product they need to build and a stable spec. You'll find that the team can produce a quality implementation much faster than they would otherwise.

So why don't all startup teams do this? Because we're such an engineering-driven industry that we just naturally start there. But any startup has to realize that everything starts with the right product, so the first order of business is to figure out what that is before burning through $500K or more in seed funding.

This model applies beyond startups to much larger companies as well. The difference is that bigger companies are generally able to underwrite the several iterations it takes to get to a valuable product, while startups often can't. But there's no reason for the inefficiencies that larger companies regularly endure.

So on your next startup or new product development effort, give this approach a try.

Chapter 30:

INNOVATING IN LARGE COMPANIES

Difficult But Worth The Effort

There is a lot of cynicism out there about whether or not you can really innovate in a big company. Some believe that nearly all true innovation happens in the startup environment, and that the best a large company can do is either copy those innovations or acquire the successful startups. While I agree that it is certainly much easier to innovate in a startup, innovation most definitely can happen in larger companies as well.

Unless you've worked at one of these large companies, you might be surprised to hear that innovation is actually a problem. After all, we hear so much about it—and see the success of large technology companies—we naturally assume that innovation is powering all this growth. But as we explained earlier, as organizations get larger, they invariably become more conservative, and less willing to take risks. Again, this is because large companies have much more to lose than smaller companies, so they get really good at protecting what they have. But there are also substantial advantages to shipping product from a large company and, despite their risk-averse nature, your company does need you to innovate.

The two biggest factors influencing your ability to innovate in a large company are your corporate culture and your manager. In my experience, there is much that the typical large company could do to improve the ability of their employees to innovate.

So, what can you do if you find yourself in a team and an organization where innovation seems difficult? Here are several techniques for coming up with the innovations your product is looking for:

Innovation via the 20% Rule

Many of you have heard that at Google, engineers get to spend 20% of their time on the projects of their choice. More than 20 years ago, this was also the policy for our team at HP Labs, and we borrowed the idea from Xerox PARC. It worked then and it still works now. At HP Labs, our job was to come up with innovative technologies that the product divisions could then incorporate into commercial products. In the group I was in, we took five new products to market, and only one of them was for a technology that came from above (and that product was the one that actually failed badly in the market). The other four innovations were fruits of the 20% rule.

As much as we might like to think that the great product ideas are the result of great strategic planning, or that they come down from the executive team, in many cases, the best ideas come from the bottom up. What's great about the 20% rule is that lots of ideas can be tried out. And when you inject the feeling of ownership that comes from thinking up the ideas yourselves, the ideas are pursued with more passion and creativity.

If your company has the 20% rule, make sure it applies to product managers and interaction designers as well as to engineers. Unfortunately, most companies don't have the 20% rule. That's a shame, and I hope you bring this up and that management decides to give it a try. But if not, that's why skunk works was invented...

Innovation via Skunk Works

Skunk works is a very old industry term that originally referred to secret military projects, but today refers to chasing ideas under the radar, unhampered by bureaucracy, on your own time if necessary. Skunk works projects have saved countless large companies.

In large organizations, it's hard to get permission to officially explore ideas. However, once you have proven an idea, it's remarkably easy to get the project funded. So long as you continue to carry out your official job responsibilities, management is usually supportive—many times they'll even pitch in and help.

Just remember that your company likely owns the intellectual property of anything you come up with on the job, so I'm not suggesting that this is how you pursue your new startup idea. If you do decide to chase a skunk works idea, and the result looks good but your company doesn't want to pursue for whatever reason, you might want to discuss an arrangement where you pursue the idea on your own. Those of you that know your Silicon Valley history may recognize this situation as the birth of Apple Computer when Steve Wozniak's employer HP wasn't ready to enter the personal computer market.

Innovation via Observation

One of the easiest ways I know of to innovate is to just watch (and listen) as actual users attempt to use your current product or a competitor's product. Watch a few of these sessions and you'll start to see patterns of frustration and expectation. Watch some more and you'll start to get ideas of how to better meet the needs. Bring in an engineer who is familiar with the available technologies, and together you will start to come up with better ways of solving the problem.

The key is to get the product in front of actual target users, not early adopters, and not anyone from your company (including you). You don't need formal usability testing labs either. You can do this informally, and you can often take the software out to the users (ideally in their native habitat—their office, their home, or the mall).

And you don't just care about whether the software is usable or not. You care about whether or not the software is meeting their needs. Even if it's usable, do they care? What problem do they really need solved?

Remember: innovation is rarely about solving an entirely new problem. More often it is solving an existing problem in a new way. So watching people struggle with their existing solutions is a great way to highlight innovation opportunities.

Innovation via User Experience Design

Another good source of innovation is to step back, relax your technical constraints for a moment, and consider what the ideal user experience would be for your product. Not just more efficient implementation of tasks, but eliminating tasks altogether. What is really essential, and what is there just because it's a side effect of the way the product is designed and built?

Every system has an implementation model that is the basis for how the product was built. But the user doesn't think this way—he has a conceptual model in mind for how he wants to think about this problem, and what he expects the system to present. Frustration happens when the user is presented not with something that reflects his conceptual model, but instead reflects the implementation model.

When you spot these incongruences, you have identified an opportunity for innovation (or at the very least, an opportunity for significant product improvements).

Innovation via Acquisition

Finally, we do need to talk about innovation via acquisition. Many product managers view an acquisition as a failure on their part. But in truth, acquisition can be an excellent technique for innovation— especially in areas where the risks are high. In essence, the company lets dozens of startups test the waters, try out their ideas, and either succeed or fail. The few remaining companies with products that work out may be good candidates for acquisition. Not only does this sort of acquisition bring in innovative new technologies, but they also bring in new blood with new ideas that you can leverage for your own purposes.

I encourage product managers at large companies to reach out and establish relationships with interesting, related startups. You can often help—and learn from—one another, and the nurturing you do might just save your company millions. There are many cases where the company that was acquired did not choose the highest bid, but instead the company that had the people they wanted to work with.

It is important that acquisitions are handled well—as we all know most aren't. And realize that innovation via acquisition is a powerful tool for large companies to keep expanding their offerings and maintaining leadership in their markets.

I hope you'll try out some of these techniques—your company truly does need you to innovate. Peter Drucker said "Every organization needs one core competence: innovation." Innovation can absolutely happen in large companies. If you're still not convinced, just take a look at www.apple.com/iphone.

CHAPTER 31: Succeeding in Large Companies | **169**

Chapter 31:
SUCCEEDING IN LARGE COMPANIES

Top 10 List

Many of the companies I work with are quite big, and countless product leaders in these companies ask: "How do I get things done in a large company?" I have worked in several large companies and, while it's not easy, I believe that those who figure out how to leverage the considerable resources of their company bring a substantial advantage to their product.

For those of you not currently in a large company, as your company grows, you'll likely face these issues too. And if you partner with a big company, you are effectively in the same boat. You'll get more out of the relationship if you understand how these companies work.

But before we get to the specific techniques for getting your product designed, built and launched—there are two important points to understand:

First, it's critical to realize that an underlying dynamic in large organizations is that they are generally risk averse. This is not an accident—it's because large companies have much more to lose than smaller companies, and it's one of the biggest cultural changes that comes with success and growth. It's also why it's so much easier to innovate in a small company. So first and foremost, you need to realize that you will have to deal head-on with the many mechanisms that large companies put in place to protect what they have accumulated. Start by memorizing this paragraph.

Second, many of these same organizations have at least some degree of matrix management and shared resources, where key members of the product team (most often design, engineering, QA, site operations, and marketing), are shared resources, and your project needs to secure the necessary people from the pool in order to staff up and create your product. It's not that this organizational design is particularly effective, it's just that this model has significant cost savings over project-oriented approaches (where much like a startup, you assemble a dedicated product team for the life of the project).

With these points in mind, here is a list of ten techniques for getting things done in a large company:

1. Learn how decisions are really made in your organization.

Every organization is different. The key is to learn and accept how things get done in your organization. Don't try to change the culture. If you want to succeed in your company, you'll need to embrace it. Learn to love it. And be sure you look closely. Despite any formal decision processes that may exist, don't be surprised if your company requires one key person (or a few) to buy off on any significant decision. If this is the case, at least you know who you really need to convince, and then you can work on the best way to reach that person. And you'll need to learn how that person makes decisions, for example, does she base her decisions on a demo, or market data, or on customer commitments and testimonials?

2. Build relationships before you need them.

If you prefer to go it alone, you might want to consider a startup, as large companies are all about people working with and depending on each other. You need to figure out all the people across the company that you might have to depend on to get your product designed, built, and launched. It'll probably be a long list. But well before you need the help of these people, you should introduce yourself, ask how you can best work with them, and start getting them excited about what you're working on. Try to figure out if there's anything you can do to help them in their job. Make friends.

3. Long live *skunk* works.

It really is easier to beg forgiveness than ask permission, especially in larger companies (see the point above about risk aversion). If you have a product idea, you can create a PowerPoint presentation and propose it through the proper channels, but it's all too likely that the idea won't go anywhere. However, if you take that idea—along with a few like-minded friends from across the company—and you flesh the idea out into a prototype, then if the idea is a good one, you'll be stunned at how quickly the resources of the company will line up to help. Countless great products were launched this way. More on this point in the chapter on innovation, but for now, know that your idea will have a much better chance of getting traction if you can actually show the idea works, rather than just talking about it.

4. Just get it done.

One of the great ironies of large companies is that even though there may be thousands of employees, it can often be impossible to get someone to help when you need them. Even when management is very willing and supportive, there may be no suitable resources available. In this case, you may need to get creative. You might, for example, be able to find some funding for a contractor, or call in some favors, or you might have to pitch in yourself. In a large company with formal processes and deliverables required, it may be easier to step in and perform the task or create the deliverable yourself rather than fight the process. I know of many cases where the product manager needed to help out with deliverables for customer support, sales training, technical writing, QA, engineering, and marketing. You have to be willing to do whatever it takes.

5. Pick your battles.

The most effective people in a large organization have far more friends than enemies. Getting things done in a big company isn't easy, and there will be many situations where you'll have good reason to be frustrated, but you need to pick your battles carefully. Make sure you pick something worth fighting for, where the outcome truly matters, so that if any bridges are burned it's worth it. And when you do fight, make sure you're fighting for your product and not against another person. Try to bring the company along with you and not back your adversaries into a corner. You don't want to win the battle only to lose the war.

6. Build consensus before important meetings where decisions are required.

Always keep in mind than once someone opposes your position in a broad and public way, you have a major problem. It will not be easy for that person to publicly switch positions. In the long run, it takes much less time to build consensus beforehand when the outcome is important. In a large company, the main value of these decision meetings is for everyone to see everyone else in the same room indicate their support for your product or decision. So make sure that before any big meeting (or before sending out an important e-mail), you take some time to talk one on one with each person who will attend to ensure they have a chance to privately voice any concerns to you. You can then address their concerns directly, and get them on board and willing to indicate this publicly.

7. Be smart about how you spend your time.

It is all too easy in a big company to get sucked into a week full of non-stop meetings. At the end of the week, you will have rushed from meeting to meeting and stayed up late trying to keep up with your e-mail, but you will not have actually done the things that will make a real difference to your product. Triage your meetings ruthlessly. Attend the meetings you must, but get used to trusting your colleagues to do their jobs and know that they'll let you know if something really needs your attention. Most importantly, make sure you have the time during the week to work on the items crucial to the success of your product: your product strategy, your roadmap, the current prototype of the next release, your understanding of the competition and—especially—talking to actual users and customers.

8. Share information.

Communication is hard in any organization. In a large company, however, communication is a serious challenge, and information becomes a kind of currency. Unfortunately, many people actually do treat it like currency, and hoard it rather than sharing it freely. Don't take the view that information is power. You have more to gain by sharing it, and hopefully others will reciprocate and help keep you informed as well. So anything you can do to help your colleagues by providing useful information as soon as you get it is good for you—and good for your company.

9. Put your manager to work.

In a large company, your manager can make a big difference to your success. Assuming your manager is reasonably well regarded, you should leverage his or her relationships, and use your manager to get a better understanding of the company and your management chain. Make it easy for your manager by doing your homework and providing the information he or she needs to make your case to others. Make sure your manager knows he or she can trust you talking to all levels of the organization.

10. Evangelize!

In a large company, the need to evangelize never stops. You need to continuously spread the word, explain the vision and strategy, demo the prototype, and share customer feedback. Don't underestimate the importance of this internal sales function. Make sure everyone even remotely connected with your product understands why the product is important, and how they can help.

While it is undeniably hard to overcome the internal obstacles and get the considerable resources of a large company focused on your product, the benefits can be tremendous. You will get a level of attention from the press, industry analysts, partners, customers, and users that the small company can't buy at any price. So it definitely pays for you to learn how to use the assets of your company to the fullest.

A great closing quote on this topic from my friend David Weiden, which I think sums up nicely the situation and opportunity for many people in large companies: "Most people wander around in the dark and bitch about it being dark, instead of learning where the light switches are."

DILBERT: © Scott Adams/Dist. by United Feature Syndicate, Inc.

In Search Of Inspiring Products

What exactly makes a product inspiring? In this section we consider the characteristics of inspiring and successful products, and discuss the keys to creating them.

Chapter 31:
LESSONS FROM APPLE

A Different Type Of Hardware Company

I have to admit to a strong bias up front: I love Apple. I think they're responsible for some of the best technology products our industry has produced in the past 25 years, and I have been a fan of the company ever since the Lisa (which I consider a prototype for the Mac) was introduced to the public in 1983. I view Steve Jobs as one of the best product managers of all time.

Recently, the Apple iPhone made its debut, and once again they have redefined the industry. But when I talk to people about that product, and Apple in general, I'm struck by how many different opinions there are as to what accounts for their success.

I strongly disagree with those who attribute their success to marketing prowess (although I think they're quite good at marketing).

To explain, let's take a look at the iPhone. Not so much about the specifics of it, but why I think Apple is able to consistently redefine major consumer markets—whether personal computers, digital music players, or cell phones.

There is a great deal to learn from Apple, but to me there are three higher-order lessons:

1. The Hardware Serves the Software

Unlike virtually every other hardware company, Apple understands that the role of the hardware is to serve the software, and not the other way around. The software needs to know what the user wants the phone to do, so hardware technologies like multi-touch displays, and accelerometer and proximity sensors are invented to enable this. Every technology is there for a purpose. That said, while the hardware and software technology are truly impressive, Apple understands that once you get beyond the early adopters, that's not what people care about. Which leads to the next point...

2. The Software Serves the User Experience

Almost every consumer company out there today gives lip service to the user experience, but Apple means it. Usability, interaction design, visual design, industrial design, are all front and center in the company's priorities—and it shows. It may have taken two-and-a-half years to come up with the iPhone, but the team knew that it was all about the user experience, and they knew they had to move mountains to make the experience great. In addition, they had the talent and persistence at all levels of the company to make this happen. Contrast this with the now famous example of Microsoft's effort to make even a very minor—and long overdue—user experience improvement in Vista. However, as fundamental as the user experience is, Apple understands that...

3. The User Experience Serves the Emotion

If Apple has a secret sauce as a technology company, I believe it's this: They understand better than anyone else the role that emotion plays in getting consumers to crave, buy, and love a product. They know how to create products that speak to these emotions in consumers. People are craving the iPhone. $400 for a phone? No problem, because consumers aren't comparing the iPhone to a Razr or a Treo—it's in an entirely different league. Take a look around an airport lounge—people treat their PC like a rental car, but they coddle their Mac like it's their dream car. And, if you're brave enough, just try to take a teen's iPod away from him.

There are well over a hundred different cell phones available, but it's hard to find people that actually love their phone. They get frustrated dealing with voice mail systems that haven't improved in decades, incompatible address books, unusable Web browsers, and e-mail hacks. Apple comes along with a product that speaks directly to these unmet needs. The same thing happened with digital music players.

It's amazing to me how few companies get these points. Even the many companies that are just trying to copy, only think to copy the functionality, and don't copy what's really important.

Chapter 32:

BEWARE OF SPECIALS

Don't Fall Down This Slippery Slope

How many times have you seen the situation where a sales rep brings to the CEO a proposal from a prospect that says, "If you will just add these seven features to your product, then we'll buy your software." Or, lest anyone thinks that this situation is unique to enterprise software companies, for consumer internet service companies, your ad salesperson comes over and says that "A big prospective partner will sign a seven-figure advertising and sponsorship deal with us if you'll just agree to these site integration and placement requirements."

Either way, these are what are known as *specials*. A special is when a company gets a big check from a prospective customer or partner with the condition that you build into your product exactly what they say.

It is entirely understandable why large customers and partners may seek this arrangement. And if you're a small company that's strapped for cash, it's also very understandable that your CEO might be more than a little inclined to agree. After all, you want to be "market-driven" and you're probably going to be adding these features at some point anyway, so why not let the customer underwrite them?"

So what's wrong with doing a special? One of the surest ways to derail a product company is to confuse customer requirements with product requirements.

I've talked in several chapters about the reasons why you can't count on customers to describe the product that they need, but to summarize: first, it's extremely difficult for the customer to know what he needs until he sees it; second, customers don't know what's possible; and third, customers don't often interact with each other in order to identify common themes.

But, more generally, even if the customer doesn't have these issues, it's not clear that these are the best things to focus on right now. By pursuing these special features now, what important work are you delaying? What is the business cost of that delay?

Assuming these are not issues, specials are still dangerous. How come? Because your job is to meet the needs of a broad range of customers—that's what distinguishes product companies from customer software shops. If a year from now the market changes, you need to be able to quickly change and adapt. If you are contractually obligated to keep supporting a specific way of doing things, then your business will not be as nimble as it needs to be. Remember that every version of your product will have to be built, maintained, tested, released, documented, and supported. It doesn't take too many specials to weigh down a company to the point where it takes them months to do even the smallest release.

Don't get me wrong—there's nothing wrong with custom software shops. They provide an essential service for countless companies that need specialized solutions, and can often deliver that specialized solution in a fraction of the time and at a fraction of the cost of in-house developed solutions. But custom software is a very different business than commercial product software.

So how do you avoid the pitfalls of specials? Undeniably, it takes corporate discipline to be able to recognize specials for what they are and be willing to walk away. This leadership comes from the CEO, but there is much you can do as product manager to help.

First, it is natural for any customer to want to describe their problem in terms of the solution they can envision rather than the underlying problem itself. But as product manager it's your job to work with the customer to tease out the core issues and needs. You can help them recognize that there may be other approaches to this problem that provide a solution they would like even better. Most customers do not want to be running on a custom version of software. They want to be running on your mainstream product—the one that gets the most attention, support and improvement.

Second, consider looking at how you could keep your product general purpose but allow the product to be tailored/customized/ extended by the customer or by a solutions provider. And then have ready the names of a couple of system integrator/solution provider companies that can tailor your product to meet this specific need. You may need to partner with the solution provider so that your customer doesn't have to manage two relationships and have to worry about finger pointing if there are issues.

So far, my examples have mainly been in the enterprise software space. But the problem of specials is becoming increasingly severe in the consumer Internet services space where—for many companies—advertising that is not aligned with the site's objectives has significantly distracted or even damaged the user experience.

For many advertisers, the main objective is very simply to move traffic from your site to their site. If this isn't your goal, you've got a strategic conflict. For some sites—such as directories or search engines—this is fine, but for others, you end up trading short-term traffic for your site's future. This really isn't in anyone's best interest.

I have found advertisers to be willing and interested in finding better, more synergistic ways to work together. When you have a strategy—and a clear role for them—they are more than willing to work with you. They know that old-style Internet advertising is of limited value, and they want something better as much as you do.

Whether it's enterprise software or consumer Internet services, it's the product manager's job to ensure that you're building the right product, and that the product will be applicable to and usable by a wide range of customers.

 ### WHAT ABOUT REQUIREMENTS MANAGEMENT TOOLS?

There are several vendors that offer a category of tool called "requirements management software." These tools are aimed at helping product managers and product marketing gather, track, prioritize and report customer requirements.

While these tools have been offered for several years, I rarely find them in use, but I do sometimes get asked about these tools and if I recommend them in general.

While I am all for tools that help people do their jobs better, the problem is that, while these tools are well intentioned, they make it extremely easy to fall into the trap of confusing customer requirements with product requirements.

In the worst case, they institutionalize the misguided practices that are responsible for so many bad products.

In the best case, they can help automate what most product managers already do with Word, Excel or a project Wiki.

The thing is, in most cases the Wiki works just great, so there's little need for expensive software with its own learning curve that just ends up distracting you from the real thinking that must go on in order to come up with a winning product.

Chapter 34:
THE NEW OLD THING

What Is Possible Is Constantly Changing

With apologies to one of my favorite authors Michael Lewis (see *The New New Thing*), in this chapter I talk about a common misconception among product managers and companies in general.

Many companies believe they need to create an entirely new market in order to do something big. The media helps fuel this. Everyone wants to know: "What's going to be the next new thing?"

While it's always fun to speculate on what the next new big thing is, much more often than not, the next big thing is not something altogether new, but rather a new incarnation of something old. The difference is that the new product does it so much better, faster, and/ or cheaper that they end up redefining their category.

Let's look at some examples: When Google entered the search market, many people scoffed because they considered the market mature, with dozens of search engines already out there (remember AltaVista, Infoseek, and Snap?). The difference was that Google actually provided useful results. Consistently. So much so that they soon came to define the category.

Similarly, while there were literally over a hundred MP3 players on the market when Apple introduced the *iPod*, the product was so much better that they quickly redefined the category.

There are two key methods that smart companies use to create winning products in mature markets.

First, they understand their target market and where the current products fall short. Product usability testing is my favorite technique for doing this, and you can do this with your competitor's products in addition to your own.

Second, great product leaders know that what is now possible is always changing. New technologies enable new solutions that may not have been possible or feasible until now. It is not easy to constantly stay on top of relevant technologies and consider how they might be applied to help solve the problems you face, but it can make all the difference for your product.

Remember: great product managers combine what is desirable with what is just now possible. Apple and Google understand this. Product opportunities exist everywhere, in virtually every market. But you must identify the need, and then search for new ways of applying technology to solve the problem.

The End Of Innovation?

Recently I was doing an interview with a member of the press having to do with the future of Silicon Valley, and I was asked this question: "Do you think there are any good opportunities left?" It took me a minute to realize that he meant this as a serious question. The whole concept seems so foreign to me, especially since I personally see more opportunity now than I have ever seen before.

But the question caused me to think about why I believe this so strongly. For anyone that has any doubts at all, I'd say three things:

First, as long as there are products that drive you nuts, there are opportunities for someone to do it better. How about a cell phone that doesn't drop calls? How about a home computer that your parents can actually administer without your help?

Second, what is possible is always changing. Just because something isn't feasible today doesn't mean it won't be tomorrow.

Third, today's applications are tomorrow's foundation. That's how things work in our business. Initially, the browser was an application to look at some content on a Web site. Today the Internet is a foundation enabling applications like eBay, Skype, and PayPal.

Likewise, until recently, most people viewed Facebook as a social networking application, but now it is a foundation for a new wave of Internet applications.

There's no way that all the good opportunities are gone. In fact, there are more products I'd like to be working today than ever before.

Chapter 35:

FEAR, GREED AND LUST

The Role Of Emotion In Products

I find it ironic that so many of us in the product world come from science- and business-oriented backgrounds, yet such a large part of what we do every day is really all about emotion and human psychology. Most of us may not think of our job this way, but we should.

People buy and use products largely for emotional reasons. The best marketing people understand this, and the best product people ensure that their products speak to these emotions.

In the enterprise space, the dominant emotion is generally fear or greed. If I don't buy this product, my competitors will beat me to market, hackers will penetrate my firewalls, or my customers will desert me. Or, if I do buy this product, I will make more money, save more money, or stop spending so much money.

In the consumer space, the dominant emotions get more personal. If I buy this product or use this Web site, I will make friends (loneliness), find a date (love or lust), win money (greed), or show off my pictures or my taste in music (pride).

You may not have thought about your product or service in these terms before, but if you apply this emotional lens, you can start to view things much more in line with how your users and customers view your service—and potential competitors. Where else can they go to get these needs met? What could be done to the visual design to speak more directly to these emotions? What features can we provide that speak more directly to these emotions? What features get in the way of clearly speaking to these emotions?

Keep in mind also that different types of users may bring different emotional needs to the table. An eBay power seller is not the same as a buyer looking for a great bargain, or a buyer looking for the thrill of competing with others to "win" an item.

When you do prototype testing with your target users, after you determine whether or not the test subject can actually figure out how to use the product or service, you should take the opportunity to essentially do a one-on-one focus group to try to learn what emotion is driving this user, and how well your product meets that emotional need.

You can hopefully see why user experience design (interaction and visual design) and usability testing play such a key role in coming up with a winning product.

Once you have clearly identified and prioritized the dominant buying emotions your customers bring to your product, focus on that emotion and ask yourself where else they might be able to get that need met? That's your real competition. In many cases you'll find that the competition you should be worrying about is not the startup or big portal that's after the same thing you are, but rather the offline alternative.

Chapter 35:

THE EMOTIONAL ADOPTION CURVE

An Interview With Jeff Bonforte

In his book, *Crossing the Chasm*, Geoffrey Moore introduces the powerful notion of a technology adoption curve, comprised of innovators and early adopters, followed by the early majority, the late majority and, finally, the laggards. He goes on to explain how few products get beyond the early adopters (they fall into the chasm).

Jeff Bonforte—as of this writing an exec at Yahoo! responsible for several industry-leading products used by millions—argues for adding a layer of analysis to the technology adoption curve, based on the driving emotions of the users in each group.

In this interview, Jeff shares his views on the role of emotions in product development.

Marty: Why do you like to focus on anger?

Jeff: Because angry people dictate the future of technology.

I like my product managers to focus on the most miserable thing people have to deal with everyday. If you can solve that problem, that actually changes behavior, and that can lead to the truly big product wins.

Don't focus on the technology of your product, just think about the people that you're trying to help. What are the problems they're dealing with? What are the things that they're frustrated with?

For example, every single one of us hates to travel nowadays—its just miserable. It's almost as if it's engineered for misery from start to finish. Or, we hate our telephone company—it's almost impossible not to. They send us a bill that's so complicated and so structured to screw you over. The rules are so elaborate that almost nobody understands them. The result is you feel like the entire billing process was engineered from the start to screw you over, and you're in a monthly battle to figure out how not to get screwed.

In my view, far too many product managers talk in terms of features and technology, and we don't really talk in terms of the user's core needs or emotions.

Marty: Let's go back to the technology adoption curve. What do you see as the underlying emotions and needs driving each of the groups of users?

Jeff: In the Technology Adoption model, we're told that there's a technology adoption curve, and it's nice and clean. But there's also a chasm, and maybe there's a tornado in there too. But, what does that mean exactly? What are we supposed to do to design around these things?

Instead of thinking about these groups using the labels that we were given by Geoffrey Moore—which, by the way, I found to be counterintuitive—I instead assign one of the emotional states for their adoption of technology. So, I talk about the Lover, the Irrational, the Efficient, the Laugher, and the Comfortable.

Marty: What does each of these groups represent?

Jeff: The Lovers (Innovators) are the techies who buy the product because they find the technology cool. These people are very dangerous to product managers because they are driven by very different needs than the larger population. They look at solving tough technical problems as fun.

On the other hand, the Irrationals (Early Adopters) feel the same emotions as the general population, but with more intensity. These are often negative emotions such as anger, fear, or loneliness, but in any case, the strength of these feelings can lead to buying behavior that is not economically rational, for example, they'll spend more time learning something than the value they get just so they can get the satisfaction of addressing these emotional needs.

The good news is that as the product improves, ordinary people who feel the more subdued versions of the same emotions will also be motivated to buy.

The Efficients (Early Majority) will adopt when the technology becomes practical. Again, they feel the same emotion, but they're more pragmatic about the benefits versus the costs.

The Laughers (Late Majority, and Yahoo's core constituency) feel the same emotion, but it's more muted and they don't want to deal with any grief in order to get the benefits.

The Comfortable (Laggards) are the 15% that want the benefits but it just has to be drop dead simple and convenient for them to make the move.

In this view of adoption, there is tremendous power in the Irrationals.

Lovers and Irrationals are often coming in the door at the same time, despite the traditional adoption curve that seems to imply there's first one and then the other. While Lovers and Irrationals may enter in at the same time, Lovers are the worst possible people in the world from a product manager's perspective.

Marty: Why is that?

Jeff: Because they mislead you one hundred percent of the way. Lovers buy a Prius because they like the battery technology.

On the other hand, Irrationals buy a Prius because they love the environment so much that they'll spend $22,000 over the benefit of the environment. They could just buy carbon credits and carbon neutralize themselves, or they could get a motorcycle, but they overspend on the solution because they're passionate about the problem they're trying to solve.

The bottom line is that Irrationals are really interesting, and Lovers are really not.

People that obsess over your product because they like battery technology don't buy your product for the same reasons anyone else does, but the Irrationals do.

Irrationals are essentially overreacting to the anger, but the emotional reaction they have is more of a multiplier times their logic. They exaggerate the value. But if you can tap into what they're thinking and what they feel, this can be very powerful.

The Irrationals can teach you the value of your product all the way down the line.

The latent frustration is highest amongst the Irrational and then it dissipates, but it's still always there. The Lovers are largely unconcerned with the core solution—they're more concerned with the technology involved.

One of the reasons startups in particular fall into the chasm is that they misread the situation—they confuse the Irrationals with the Lovers.

Marty: So how do you address this at Yahoo!?

Jeff: One of the challenges Yahoo! and many large companies face is that we envy a lot of startups, and we think, "We want to do cool stuff like that." But Yahoo has made its fame and fortune off serving the Laughers, so we will serve our user base much better by understanding Irrationals, and not by kowtowing to the Lovers.

Sometimes marketing folks confuse the emotional groups with demographics. They'll look at the Irrationals and say, "Oh, this group is comprised of males 18-30," but it's not true. If you're in finance, you may have an Irrational group that's very different looking—it could be retired women. You have to look at each product individually, and look at the core emotions for this particular product.

Marty: So what do teach your product managers to look for?

Jeff: Look for anger, exasperation, and frustration. If you just take a look at all those we love to hate—the telcos, banks, consumer credit firms, the tax man, government bureaucracy, airlines, health-care—these are all great opportunities for innovation because the consumer latent frustration is so high.

Look at the music industry. We have to pay $15.98 for a CD with one good song on it. Is it any surprise that so many people feel good about stealing from these people?

We're all so impressed with Skype's growth, and yet, had we looked and seen the latent anger and frustration in the space, it would have been relatively predictable to say, it's not about standards or technology, or being open versus proprietary. The Skype guys rejected all that thinking and said we're just gonna make it work, and they then tapped into that latent frustration. It was like heroin, you couldn't stop it.

Contrast this with the webcam business. The problem here is there's no angry person in the webcam business—we don't hate our webcam providers, or our video conferencing guys—and webcam satisfies a need that's high up in Maslow's pyramid. It's "I wanna see my kid," and while there's love involved there, not all of us have kids, and you can easily call your kids, so we're not all dying for a webcam.

So, when you add video to Skype, not much happens. Their user base doesn't grow that much, the usage of webcam and messenger doesn't go down—nothing changed. And so the chasm for webcam is actually huge because taking it to the mainstream for webcam means you don't have much frustration to leverage—you don't have that driving emotional need.

You really need the Irrationals to slingshot your business into the Efficients and the Laughers. Without that emotion from those irrational people you don't get the passion that carries the product over the chasm. So as with so many things in life we're brought back to Maslow's pyramid. If you look at the needs, the further down you go, the more you're tapping into core emotions, and the better off you are because these are the deepest emotions for humans.

Politicians like to tap into the fear emotion and explain that bad people are gonna destroy your cities, or come and bomb you, or you're not going to have food tomorrow. Well it's not that hard to motivate you to change your behavior when you energize these core emotions. It's much harder to get people to do something by appealing to their aspirations.

Google is the big winner in this way of thinking because the nature of a search engine is to help address countless critical human needs. If you've been diagnosed with a disease you go to Google to learn how to treat it. If you have to buy something, Google finds it for you. They're the good guys that are there to help you with whatever problem you have.

So the question we ask is, "What are the emotions that are driving the behavior?" And then we look for ways to tap into those emotion with features and all the other things. We assess for each of our projects which core emotions they appeal to, and how acute is the user's pain.

Marty: Do you have a favorite approach for assessing these core emotions?

Jeff: One technique I use is what I call the "freshman test." Think back to the first day you walked into high school. You feel more pure emotions of human frailty in that one day than in any other day in your life. You're small, your hormones are all out of whack, anything you had acheived in your previous school completely gets washed away and you're a nobody—and you know you're a nobody.

If you can tap into any one of those emotions that every human everyday feels—loneliness, insecurity, fear, frustration, anger—some bit of that freshman thing, then you're on the right track.

Chapter 36:
USABILITY VS. AESTHETICS

Both Are Important

I think most would agree that the general state of Web site design is still in its infancy, at least as practiced by most companies. While there are some notable exceptions, many sites—even from major players—are often either very difficult to use, downright ugly, or both. I have formed some theories as to why so many sites are bad, and what it will take to make this a better world as we all spend an increasing amount of our life interacting with the Web.

I have long noted that too few companies invest the time and resources in user experience that they should. However, what I've had a harder time explaining is why companies that do invest the time and resources in user experience still often have such bad sites.

Two edge cases in particular struck me as interesting. On the one hand, so many graphic/visual design firms have beautiful, artistic sites, that are difficult to read and poorly structured. On the other hand, many interaction design firms have very usable sites that are easy to navigate and find the info you need, yet are boring, primitive, and unappealing.

I think what these two cases illustrate is that the disciplines of interaction design and visual design are very different. To have a site that is both usable and appealing you need both skills on your design team. Some teams are very lucky and they have a designer talented at both types of design. But in many cases, I think they just expect that since they hired a "designer," that person should be able to do both—and they can't.

Even worse—but most common of all—is when the company has neither type of designer, and they look to either the product manager or the UI engineer to design the site. When I talk to enterprise companies, this is unfortunately still the norm. When I talk to consumer startups, they usually have one or the other type of designer.

Many teams feel that the visual design of a product or site is not really important. They argue that what matters is the functionality and the value proposition, and that things like nice colors, fonts, icons and layout are just unnecessary and superficial fluff. I strongly disagree with this view, and the more products I see, the stronger I believe in (a) the role that emotion plays in inspiring products, and (b) the direct role visual design plays in creating that emotion.

You can show the exact same functionality to a user—one with wireframes and one with a good visual design—and the overall response can be dramatically different.

Much as product management and product marketing are different functions requiring different training and skills, interaction design and visual design are different functions requiring different training and skills.

I have oversimplified somewhat here—I haven't discussed the critical roles the product manager or usability engineers play in developing a site that is both usable and enjoyable. And if the site performs like a dog, or is riddled with bugs, or is littered with advertising, then that will of course impact the experience in a big way too.

But, fundamentally, I believe you need both interaction and visual design skill sets to deliver a good user experience, and that these people need to work closely with the product manager to define the product, which includes both the functionality and the user experience.

Chapter 37:

KEYS TO CONSUMER INTERNET SERVICE PRODUCTS

Top 10 List

I love building very large-scale consumer services. Creating products that are used and appreciated by millions of people around the world is an amazing thing. And unlike most types of products, there's nothing between you and your customer—no sales force or distribution channels to work through. You can reach your user base easily and instantly, and try ideas out in near real time. You know right away if people love or hate your new ideas.

But it's also very hard.

Below is a list of ten techniques that are especially important for large-scale consumer Internet service companies. It's a general list, meant to apply to many types of services including e-commerce, social networks, search engines, and games, as just a few examples.

1. **Usability.** In my opinion, most companies give far too little attention to this in every type of product (especially enterprise software!) but, with a consumer Internet service, there simply is no getting around that it's really all about the user experience. If you can't find a way to make your

service something that the target user can figure out how to use—and provide them with an idea of why they should use it—then you're going nowhere fast. Also remember that performance is a key factor in usability. If a page takes too long to load, people will think it's broken or just go elsewhere because the experience is bad.

2. **Personas.** When you have millions of users, there is no single "user," rather you have at least several important types of users. It's critical that you segment your users into the most important personas and consider each one separately. When you create a feature, you need to examine how each persona will value and respond to that feature. See the chapter *Personas for Product Management.*

3. **Scalability.** Weird things happen to products once millions of users start using them. Databases break, performance bottlenecks pop up all over, user interfaces become unusable. You can do some amount of load testing during QA, but I've found this only finds the easy problems. I guarantee you that you'll have surprises—and not pleasant ones. Managing scalability needs takes a collaboration of product management, design, engineering, and operations. It also takes a proactive management team that allocates a significant amount of engineering and operations resources on an ongoing basis (I generally advise 20%) to scaling the product and infrastructure. If you get to the point where everything breaks and the engineering team is telling you that the "house of cards has collapsed," you're in big trouble. The only way I know to avoid that is to pay your taxes by working on scale continuously from day one, and don't let yourself get to the brink.

4. **Availability.** Very quickly you'll find that there really is no time of the day or week or month or year that your service doesn't need to be running. I don't know of anyone that has achieved 100% availability, but I know outages are painful to everyone. The life of a consumer Internet service provider is

not for everyone. Things happen at all hours, weekday and weekends, and everyone I know in the business has their stories. You need to design-in high-availability to all of your thinking just as you need to do with scalability.

5. **Customer support.** One of the biggest (and least fun) surprises that most consumer service companies run into is customer support. Traditional models of customer support can quickly bankrupt even the best services companies. This is oversimplifying a complicated topic, but you have no alternative other than designing and building the product to absolutely minimize customer support costs—especially if you charge a fee for your service. Yet, always remember that it is not about controlling customer support costs—it is about ensuring a great customer experience.

6. **Privacy and data protection.** Consumer Internet service companies can very quickly end up with far more personal information than they ever imagined. You may be collecting this data for purely innocent purposes—such as to provide a personalized user experience. But today customer data such as e-mail addresses and credit card numbers are a very sensitive asset, and you don't want the bad press, the possible penalties, and especially the customer anger that results if that data gets into the wrong hands. You need to put the protections in place early to absolutely ensure that you are protecting the information that your customers entrusted you with. You also need to protect the actual user data from your own employees.

7. **Viral marketing.** If your product is good, your users will want to share that experience with their friends, family, and co-workers. That's absolutely what you want, but it's surprising how few companies actually do anything to facilitate this most powerful form of marketing. Consider what you can do with your product to enable users to invite their friends to try it. Also, work the numbers—most companies are willing to pay a certain amount per new

user (customer acquisition cost, usually for marketing and advertising). Maybe you can funnel some of that money to your users instead? But find ways to make sharing the love easy—even without using financial incentives.

8. **Globalization.** If you have a good service, you'll find that it will quickly spread beyond your country's borders—first to other countries that speak the same language, then to the rest of the major Internet-connected countries. It is far less expensive—and overall, faster to market—to design a product that can easily be localized than it is to try and take a product for one country/currency/language/culture and rewrite it for another. You don't have to localize initially for all the countries but—as your business spreads—you can much more rapidly and economically meet your new users' needs.

9. **Gentle deployment.** When millions of people are using your service, any change is a big deal, and every change needs to be considered carefully. We talked earlier about gentle deployment strategies (see the chapter *Gentle Deployment*), but suffice it to say here that changes need to be deployed intelligently. This doesn't just mean great QA—it also means deploying gradually, and giving your users time to switch when they have the time to learn about the changes, not when you happen to roll it out. In many cases, this involves deploying the new version alongside the old so that people can switch over a period of time. Also, do everything you can to eliminate gratuitous changes. It's hard enough for your community to absorb features that they know they want and need.

10. **Community management.** Every company is dependent on its customers, but for consumer Internet service companies, this community of users takes on even more powerful importance—they can make you or break you. It has never been easier for them to communicate how much they love your product—or how badly you just treated

them. If your users value your product, they will want to be loyal, and they will want to be a part of the great community you are creating. But they also want to be appreciated and recognized—and not just with lip service. There are many ways to reach out to your community—to learn from them and understand where they want to see your product go. There are also many ways to show your gratitude to the community and to recognize those that make especially valuable contributions. Do this, and make community awareness a top priority for everyone in your company— from the CEO on down.

If you can keep these 10 techniques in mind as you create your consumer Internet services, you'll save yourself a lot of grief. But as I said above, these are great products to work on, and it's easy to become hooked on these types of businesses.

Chapter 38:
KEYS TO ENTERPRISE PRODUCTS

Top 10 List

I'm frustrated by the state of the enterprise software industry, and I have been for quite some time. While there are some notable exceptions, I find fewer examples of good products in this space than any other. Many people view the enterprise software market as mature—or worse—but I think customers are just frustrated and aren't anxious to spend yet more money on more disappointing products. And they're just not willing to dish out hundreds of thousands—or even millions—of dollars on professional services just to get them working.

There are a number of reasons why the industry is in this state but, regardless, I believe that good product management can help improve the situation substantially.

Before I get started, let me clarify what I mean by the very general term *enterprise software*. The two key points to clarify are who the software is sold to, and what type of software product we're talking about.

Regarding who the software is sold to, the main point is that the products are sold to businesses rather than consumers. There is of course a full-spectrum of business size, and I'm intentionally not including the small office/home office/small business markets because, in my view, they're really much more like the consumer market than the enterprise market (and the reason so many companies in the past tried and failed in the huge small biz market is because they didn't realize this fact and its implications for product requirements). I do, however, include medium-size businesses in this definition even though many people reserve the term enterprise for a larger group such as the Fortune 500. But I find many of the challenges start to show with mid-size businesses.

And then there's the type of software. Enterprise infrastructure products (e.g., security software, systems management, and communications software) have some significant differences from enterprise applications (e.g., SFA, CRM, ERP), but I'll speak to both here. I think the top-10 list is essentially the same, although I'd weight the importance of each item differently based on whether it's infrastructure or application.

Here is a list of ten techniques that are especially important for enterprise software companies:

1. **Usability.** Pity the poor souls who must sit at their desks all day and use the typical enterprise applications for purchasing, billing, customer service, and hundreds of other applications. If the people who actually had to use the systems were the same ones that made the actual buying decisions, I think we'd have a very different set of vendors. I'm very sorry to say it, but most of the applications are just awful. One of my favorite books is *The Inmates are Running the Asylum* by Alan Cooper. Nowhere is his argument truer than with enterprise software. I find too few enterprise companies doing any interaction design, visual design, or usability testing—and it certainly shows. Even when the application produces business results, there is still a sour taste in the mouth, and you rarely find true enthusiasm for these types of products. It really is time to raise the bar.

2. **Product actually needs to work.** Even more egregious than poor product usability, too many enterprise products simply don't work—at least not without tremendous investments in time and money to "customize" and "integrate" or develop countless workarounds. This is certainly not the case with all products, but the many out there that ship with often hundreds of serious defects give a bad reputation to all of us. As product manager, it's essential to make sure your product does what you says it will.

3. **Specials.** One of the biggest mistakes companies make is that they think they can get their product requirements from their customers. I've talked about this earlier (see *Beware of Specials*), but the most dangerous example of this is when the sales organization brings in a potential customer that has a big check all ready to sign if you'll just agree to put these seven features in your product. Soon you're becoming a custom software shop, and you don't have anything resembling a generally useful product. If that's not bad enough, there's a good chance the initial customer won't be happy with those seven features anyway (once they got it and tried it they realized they needed something different). Avoiding specials takes a lot of discipline—especially for a small company struggling to bring in some cash—but it is critical you create products that meet the needs of a wide range of customers.

4. **Customers and Charter User Programs.** The above is not to say that you shouldn't listen to your customers—you should absolutely meet with and listen to many customers. Just don't expect them to be able to dictate your product requirements. To determine the real product requirements, you'll need to meet with many customers. One valuable technique is to identify a half-dozen or so great potential customers (smart, enthusiastic, motivated, friendly) and invite them to participate on a charter customer program (see the chapter *Charter User Programs*). In exchange for

the opportunity to work closely with the development team, they know that their needs will be understood and seriously considered, and they agree to be accessible to try out ideas, answer questions, and install software immediately—and, if it meets their needs, to be vocal reference customers. Your goal should always be to have at least half a dozen live, happy referenceable customers when you release your product.

5. **Designing for the sales channel.** It's critical to design your product around the needs of your sales and distribution channel. Different channels require different capabilities. The key is to provide value all along the distribution chain. If you're selling through systems integrators, you'll need to ensure that your product doesn't try to cut them out of the equation. If you're selling through VARs that supply a wide range of products, you'll need to ensure that your product doesn't overwhelm them with time-consuming technical requirements. Many otherwise good products struggle because they're not appropriate for their sales channel.

6. **The customer versus the user.** Many enterprise products are designed around the needs of the person who will actually buy the product—the customer. That's who the team talks to when learning about needs, and that's who has to give the okay in order to sell the product. However, as we alluded to above, there are often several different users of the product who also bring needs and requirements. For example, the different types of end-users, the systems administrators, management, and often other business applications.

7. **Product installation.** With consumer products, vendors know that they have to make the product absolutely bulletproof to install, and something that just takes minutes or even seconds. But with enterprise products, many vendors assume they'll be able to get dedicated systems administration staff that can craft custom installations that can take days or even weeks of work, and that these administrators will be able to watch over the applications

daily. Even when this is true, when the person moves on—
or is out due to vacation or illness, or just gets overloaded—
things can quickly fall apart. Again, it's time to raise the
bar.

8. **Product configuration, customization, and integration.**
An enormous professional services industry has emerged
to fill the gap and try and get these enterprise software
products to actually work, and further, to work with
each other. I believe that the vast majority of the cost
is simply due to poor product design and execution.
However, even if you accept that the need for services is
appropriate, there is still much that can be done by vendors
to make their products easier to configure, customize and
integrate. If you don't believe this is possible, look at how
Salesforce.com has redefined the game in their market.

9. **Product update.** Installing a new version of enterprise
software is never fun. The vendor thinks it's the biggest
event of the year, but the customer has a business to run,
and installing updates of vendor software isn't something
they typically want to be spending their precious time and
resources on. Having problems upgrading or requiring
complex data migration is extremely frustrating to the
customer. Again, most consumer products realize this and
make a much bigger investment in technology to upgrade,
and in testing the upgrade process.

10. **The Sales Process.** For many years, in the enterprise
software market, far too much of the sale was driven by the
talents/personality/charm of the respective sales staff. A
product selection was too often driven by the relationship
between the sales rep and the customer rather than by
whether the product was the best fit or not. While the
relationship aspects are still very important (more than
they should be), today the Internet has changed the product
research and evaluation process, and vendors need to
support this new sales process. Make your product easy to

try and buy.

If you can keep these 10 points front and center as you create your enterprise software products, you'll be far ahead of your competition—and your customers are sure to be grateful.

 ## What About Solutions Products?

I realize that most of this book is focused on the development of Internet services, and mostly consumer Internet services at that. But many product managers out there are working hard on other types of software products, such as enterprise or infrastructure software—both shipped software and hosted services.

One product area that seems to be a long-standing source of confusion for those in the industry has to do with what are referred to as *solutions products* and the associated *solutions marketing*. Just as many companies stretch the truth to call their products a *platform*, many other companies like to claim their product is a *solution*—even when it's not.

The concepts of platform and solution are both important and powerful, and those products that aren't really up to the standard just dilute the meaning for those that are and confuse the market.

Before defining a solutions product, let's first be clear on what constitutes a product in general. This may sound basic, but much software is not actually a product at all.

Here is how I characterize a *product*:

- People will pay for it; it delivers real and distinct value (and typically has its own SKU). Note that sometimes people pay by tolerating advertising, or by paying for support and not license fees, but one way or another they're compensating the provider.
- It works well in multiple customer installations. The point here is that it's not a special—this is *not* custom software.
- Your field and/or channel can effectively sell it. You provide the necessary sales tools and sales training.
- Your company will stand behind it, providing support and

adding improvements as necessary.
- Your customers and/or channel and/or services partners know how to install, configure and customize the product.

You might argue that what I'm defining here is not just a product, but a certain quality of product. And I think that's true. I consider software—even software produced by a product organization—to be just a wannabe product if it's not yet being successfully used by multiple customers. In a sense, the software has to prove its right to be considered a product, much like a platform that does not have any applications running on it isn't really much of a platform.

A *solutions product* has all of the characteristics of a product above, plus:

- The software solves a business-level problem, often for specific industry verticals.
- The product may be based on an integration of one or more component-level products, which may come from your company or from partners, and they are pre-integrated.
- If appropriate, the product is certified with partners' products as necessary (the customer needs to know the supported configurations).

I like solutions products because they speak directly to a business-level problem or need. In general, customers care much less about the underlying technology you use (other than early adopters), and more about whether you really solve their business problem. Your business problem might be disaster recovery, customer relationship management, or Sarbanes-Oxley compliance, but it isn't what flavor of the operating system is used, or what type of router you select.

Note that there are some solutions products that are turnkey, and others that require professional services. Solutions products can be for any size customer—from a single consumer to the largest enterprise—and the software may be shipped (installed) software, or software as a service.

But it's also important to point out what a solutions product is not:

- A set of instructions for how to use an existing product in a new way (customer's won't pay for that)
- A set of customizations/scripts from the field or other external source (not supportable)

There are many field or marketing organizations that can clearly see the customer demand for true solutions, but their product organization only provides the underlying component products.

The temptation is to get creative and to try to cobble together something that they hope they will have better luck selling. But while this might buy a little time, as soon as a competitor comes along with a true solutions product, the customer can easily tell the difference.

Related—but the not the same as solutions products—is *solutions marketing*. I also like solutions marketing over other forms of product marketing because solutions marketing:

- Speaks to the business-level problem, aligning products with business value
- Speaks to vertical industry segments, aligning value with a particular industry's more specific—and sometimes regulated—needs.
- Showcases live customer success stories in action, in order to prove the business value
- Shows how to leverage products, professional services and business process knowledge or best practices to achieve business results

To me the trend is very clear and has been underway for several years. Increasingly, customers are demanding products that directly address business-level needs, and they're less interested in reading and comparing a data sheet of technical specs. Good solutions products and solutions marketing speak directly to these business needs.

Chapter 39:

KEYS TO PLATFORM PRODUCTS

High Leverage But Not Easy

One of the most difficult—but highest leverage—types of product management is to define successful platforms. By platforms, I am referring to foundation software that is used by application developers to create end-user solutions. Examples include operating systems (e.g., Windows, MacOS, Palm OS), operating environments (e.g., Java, Flash), Web services (e.g., Amazon's or eBay's integration APIs), game developer platforms (e.g., XNA), and application-level platform runtimes (e.g., Facebook and Salesforce.com).

Before I go further, it's important to point out what is not a platform. There are too many so-called "platforms" out there that are really just unfinished products. The team didn't do the work required to provide a complete solution, so they market it as a platform and push the work off on the customer or a developer to finish. If you can't program the platform through some form of API, and if you don't have multiple commercial software products or services built upon your software, then you're not a platform in the sense I'm describing.

But assuming you are, then you know how difficult platform product management can be. To begin with, there are three very different constituencies:

- The application providers—the businesses that choose to use your platform to build their solution.

- The developers—those who work for the application providers and who write their software using your platform services.

- The end-users—the ones who run the application provider's products, and ultimately use your services.

Each of these three constituencies brings to the table very different needs and requirements. You simply can't be a successful platform without meeting the key needs across all three.

The application provider is going to be concerned with business viability—their viability if they use your services, and your viability in case you go out of business or discontinue support for the platform. The application provider cares about your pricing, licensing, quality, support, and global availability, among other factors.

The developers are looking for services that make it easy for them to quickly create maintainable, reliable code in the languages they want to use, working with their favorite tools and infrastructure, on the devices they need to deliver on.

The end-users care mainly about the end result. If the features and services they want aren't there or don't work in the way they need, they don't buy the application, and the application provider fails. You lose a customer, and eventually you fail too.

One of the biggest mistakes platform product managers make is in the prioritization of the three constituencies. Developers are the most vocal group and the easiest for the company to relate to, so they usually get considered first. The application provider is the one writing the check, so they come close behind. But the end-user is often so far removed from the platform provider that they rarely interact directly. Unfortunately, this is precisely the reverse of what's needed. It is a big (but common) mistake to optimize for developers over the end-user.

I know this may sound heretical, but it is okay for the developers to work a little harder if the application is something end-users like and use, versus making the developers happy but nobody wants the end result.

Countless platform-wannabes made this mistake. The reasoning is very simple: I'm a developer—I know what other developers want, so I'll create something to help both my colleagues and myself. I would have to include client-side Java in this camp—great development environment, terrible user experience, terrific opportunity for Macromedia (now Adobe).

Many extremely successful platforms have been downright awful for the developers. But they succeeded because of compelling value to the end-users and—therefore—to the application providers. You don't have to look further than early Windows for an example of this.

I'm not advocating platforms that make life miserable for developers, but product management is all about choices and priorities, and it's essential to understand that the delivered application is what matters the most.

There are other important dimensions to platform product management that make this area challenging. For example, there are many different delivery models (e.g., embedded, private-label, co-branded, hosted) and many forms of customization that may be required (e.g., end-user, customer's IT, solution provider/SI, vendor, source code). Each of these is a topic in itself.

Support is also very difficult for platform providers. The bar is high because you're a critical dependency for all of your customers. That said, the great thing about working on platforms is that they're very high leverage—if you do it well, you can create a thriving ecosystem where you and your application provider partners succeed together.

SUMMARY

DILBERT: © Scott Adams/Dist. by United Feature Syndicate, Inc.

In this section we highlight the most important points and best practices for creating inspiring products, and describe how you can learn more about the topics discussed in this book.

Chapter 40:
BEST PRACTICES SUMMARY
Top 10 List

In my more than 20 years of industry experience, I have observed many practices used to create successful and inspiring products— here are what I consider to be the 10 most important.

Each is described in detail elsewhere in the book, but this summary will hopefully give you a sense of what I consider the most important practices, and I hope you'll give them all a try.

1. **The role of product management.** Too many product leaders spend their time on other activities, especially product marketing and/or project management. These activities are not a substitute for true product management.

2. **The role of user experience.** For most software products, the user experience is all-important. Devising a good user experience requires that you collaborate closely with an interaction designer and an engineer to come up with something that is valuable, usable, and feasible.

3. **Opportunity assessments.** These lightweight, to-the-point assessments replace the old "MRD" (market requirements documents). Before you jump into the solution, this makes sure you know what problem you're trying to solve, who you're trying to solve it for, and how you'll know if you are

successful.

4. **Charter user program.** It is shocking to me how many product teams think they can come up with great products without talking to users and customers. If you only do this one thing, it will ensure that you do several other things right, starting with direct and intense user interaction.

5. **Product principles.** Product management is all about making choices, and many of the techniques here are about helping you make good choices. The product principles help you identify and prioritize what you believe is important.

6. **Personas.** Another key technique for making the difficult choices required for an inspiring product is to use personas as a way to focus your release and to understand the key behaviors and underlying emotions of the target users.

7. **Focus on discovery.** The primary responsibility of the product manager is to discover a product that is valuable, usable, and feasible. It makes no sense to proceed to building something until you have evidence that you have discovered this product.

8. **The use of prototypes.** One of the most important product discovery techniques is to create a high-fidelity prototype. We do this for several reasons: First, it forces you to think much deeper about the solution; second, it enables you test your ideas out with real users; and third, it is the most useful way to describe the product to be built to the rest of the product team.

9. **Test prototype with target users.** Once you have a prototype, you can find out which of your ideas works and which do not. The techniques for this prototype testing are something that all product managers and designers need to master. Knowing how to get feedback on product ideas is probably the single most important skill for product managers.

10. **Measure to improve.** The successful product manager uses data to make important decisions, especially when trying to improve an existing product. Improving a product is not about adding features that customers request; it is about analyzing the product's actual use, and then relentlessly driving the product to improve the key metrics.

Chapter 41:

PRODUCT MANAGER WORRY LIST

Top 10 List

The strong product manager is constantly obsessed with the current and future state of her product. Here are the questions she is constantly asking herself:

1. Is my product compelling to our target customer?

2. Have we made this product as easy to use as humanly possible?

3. Will this product succeed against the competition? Not today's competition, but the competition that will be in the market when we ship?

4. Do I know customers who will really buy this product? Not the product I wish we were going to build, but what we're really going to build?

5. Is my product truly differentiated? Can I explain the differentiation to a company executive in two minutes? To a smart customer in one minute? To an industry analyst in 30 seconds?

6. Will the product actually work?

7. Is the product a whole product? How will customers actually think about and buy the product? Is it consistent with how we plan to sell it?

8. Are the product's strengths consistent with what's important to our customers? Are we positioning these strengths as aggressively as possible?

9. Is the product worth money? How much money? Why? Can customers get it cheaper elsewhere?

10. Do I understand what the rest of the product team thinks is good about the product? Is it consistent with my own view?

The reason that "thinking time" is so critical each day—and why the job of product manager is so all-consuming—is that these questions require serious and ongoing consideration.

LEARNING MORE

To learn more about this topic, and to engage in an ongoing discussion with me about product discovery and creating products customers love, see the Silicon Valley Product Group site at www.svpg.com.

You will find a blog and a free newsletter containing articles on these topics and more, a list of resources, and samples and examples of the many types of artifacts and deliverables discussed in this book.

For professional product managers, we offer executive coaching, product strategy assistance, and training workshops with hands-on learning of many of the practices described in this book, combined with current and relevant examples from industry.

Find out more at www.svpg.com.

ACKNOWLEDGEMENTS

The very nature of putting together this book on sharing best practices from the industry's best product companies means that I have learned from a great many exceptional people. I have been especially fortunate to have had the chance to work with and for some of our industry's best product minds and companies. I have learned from all of these people, but some of them have made such a deep impression on me that I must thank them here.

First, my partners at the Silicon Valley Product Group. They are my colleagues now precisely because I have been so impressed with their talents and have learned so much from each of them over the years: Chuck Geiger, Martina Lauchengco, and Kyrie Robinson.

At HP, in addition to learning the value of a strong corporate and product culture, I learned a great deal from Mike Bacco, Brian Beach, Ira Goldstein and Martin Griss especially.

The genesis of this book was material that I developed at Netscape Communications along with two absolutely exceptional product leaders—Ben Horowitz and David Weiden. Netscape provided an unparalleled learning opportunity, and I gained much insight about product and leadership working for and with truly brilliant minds including Marc Andreesen, Jennifer Bailey, Jim Barksdale, Peter Currie, Eric Hahn, Basil Hashem, Mike Homer, Omid Kordistani, Keng Lim, Bob Lisbonne, Debby Meredith, Mike McCue, Danny Shader, Sharmila Shahani, Ram Shriram, Bill Turpin, and later Barry Appelman at AOL.

At eBay, I have to especially credit Marty Abbott, Josh Kopelman, Shri Mahesh, Pierre Omidyar, Lynn Reedy and Maynard Webb.

While researching this book, I also benefited from the insights of Jim Barton, Jeff Bonforte, Kevin Compton, Fred Cox, Audrey Crane, Pete Deemer, Mark Hurst, Guy Kawasaki, Amy Klement, Norm Meyrowitz, Andrew Sandler, and Bob Vallone.

Each of these people have directly influenced me and informed specific topics in this book, either by their explicit help and coaching, or from simply their leadership and actions that I was fortunate enough to witness first hand.

While my time working for these exceptional companies was an invaluable learning experience, I found that as I began working with client companies in my work as part of SVPG, I was able to benefit greatly by getting a chance to meet and work with the product leaders at many other leading companies in our industry. There are simply too many people to list, but they know who they are, and I am grateful to every one of them.

This book is based on material produced for a blog and newsletter that I have published for several years, and each and every topic was improved thanks to feedback and comments from literally thousands of product leaders from every corner of the globe. I thank everyone who has read, shared, and commented on these articles.

I also must thank Mark Coggins, Peter Economy, John Hornbaker, Benji Jasik, Cynthia Johanson, Jeff Lash, Bruce Williams and all of the people at Westminster Printing and Promotions for their very significant help in making this book as good as it can be.

Finally, those people who know the culture of the companies I've worked at understand that many very long hours were involved, and I could not have contributed to these companies without the support of my wife and children.

ABOUT THE AUTHOR

During the course of the past 20 years, Marty Cagan has served as an executive responsible for defining and building products for some of the most successful companies in the world, including Hewlett-Packard, Netscape Communications, America Online, and eBay.

Before founding the Silicon Valley Product Group to pursue his interests in helping others create inspiring and successful products through his writing, speaking, and workshops, Marty was most recently senior vice-president of product management and design for eBay, where he was responsible for defining products and services for the company's global e-commerce trading site.